Ancient Peoples and Places

ROMANIA

General Editor

DR. GLYN DANIEL

ABOUT THE AUTHOR

After receiving his doctorate from the University of Bucharest in 1938, Professor Dumitru Berciu continued his specialized studies in Vienna and Rome, before the second World War. He now occupies the Chair of Prehistoric Archaeology at the University of Bucharest, where he is also Dean of the Faculty of History, and he is departmental head of the Archaeological Institute of the Romanian Academy. An authority on European as well as Romanian prehistory, Professor Berciu has conducted many archaeological excavations in Romania which have resulted in the precise dating of several newly discovered civilizations. He is the author of numerous archaeological works, and has been a Corresponding Member of the German Institute of Archaeology since 1965.

Ancient Peoples and Places

ROMANIA

D. Berciu

73 PHOTOGRAPHS
54 LINE DRAWINGS
10 MAPS
5 TABLES

FREDERICK A. PRAEGER
Publishers
New York · Washington

THIS IS VOLUME FIFTY-SEVEN IN THE SERIES
Ancient Peoples and Places
GENERAL EDITOR: DR. GLYN DANIEL

BOOKS THAT MATTER

Published in the United States of America in 1967
by Frederick A. Praeger, Inc., Publishers
111 Fourth Avenue, New York, N.Y. 10003

Library of Congress Catalog Card Number: 66–21770
Printed in Holland

CONTENTS

ILLUSTRATIONS

FIGURES

FIGURES

FIGURES

CHAPTER I

General Background

THE GEOGRAPHICAL SETTING

ROMANIA LIES BETWEEN latitude 43° and 48° north, in the temperate zone half-way between the North Pole and the Equator. Its territory, in the centre of Europe and crossed by longitude 25° east, is in the region where south-east peninsular Europe meets south-west continental Europe. It lies at an equal distance – about 2500 km. – from the Atlantic Ocean and the Ural mountains, and is approximately the same distance from the North Cape in Norway; to the south, however, Cape Matapan in southern Greece is only about 900 km. distant. Romania is thus much nearer to the Mediterranean than to the North Pole. It has an area of 237,500 sq. km., and the population on March 15, 1966 was 19,105,056.

From its main physical features, namely the Carpathians, the Danube and the Black Sea, Romania derives a certain economic and geographical importance.

From the nature of its contours, Romania would seem to belong to the Carpathian group of countries, but its water-courses are more Danubian in character, for it is situated on the Danube, and the mouth of this great river which gives life to so many European countries actually lies within the borders of Romania; finally, its Black Sea coast-line and its climate fall within the Pontic area. It lies, in fact, at the cross-roads of Europe, and its complex and varied geographical features include elements from central, eastern and southern Europe; but although it is a transitional zone, it also constitutes a clearly-defined unit within the arc of the Carpathians and the Danube. In other words, it has a distinctively Carpatho-Danubian character.

THE HISTORICAL SETTING

The study of the strata, the rocks, the fossils, etc., has enabled geologists and palaeontologists to define the chronology of the formation of Romania from pre-Cambrian times, and through the Cretaceous era when its basic form was established by the rising of the main Carpathian mountains, although the range as a whole was only completed during the Tertiary era. The territory of Romania finally took its present form at the beginning of the Quaternary period. In the age immediately following, when a new upthrust of the Carpathians took place, glaciers formed on the mountain heights, particularly the Maramureș, Rodna Bucegi and Făgăraș mountains, where even today signs can still be found of their erosive action. Here, too, are the glacial lakes which are such a distinctive feature of Romania's mountain terrain. During the Ice Age when much of Europe was covered by the great ice-sheet, certain of its outlying extensions such as that of the Dnieper valley came close to Romania, which thereby fell within the peri-glacial zone and acquired the characteristics associated with this type of area.

During the Quaternary era the rivers continued to hollow out still deeper beds, cutting through successive levels. The lowland and the deep valleys were formed during the Holocene period, and during the Quaternary era the loess of the Danube and Tisa plains was gradually desposited.

These geological changes naturally influenced the evolution of the flora, the fauna and the climate. In the Pleistocene period, while the ice advanced and retreated, the first men appeared in this region and began to manufacture tools from the natural materials they found.

With the arrival of the Holocene period, at the beginning of which the last geological transformations took place, and after the retreat of the ice-sheets, a rather warm desert climate set in with a distinctive Mediterranean flora; gradually, however, steppe conditions prevailed and these finally gave place to a humid climate. From this time onwards, vegetation developed which was adapted to the varying conditions at different altitudes, including pines, oaks, beeches and deciduous trees generally, so that the whole of the terrain was now thickly wooded. During this period too, the final evolution of the fauna of the region took place.

There were other climatic changes during the Neolithic and early metal ages bringing with them successive phases of humidity and drought, which helped to alter the habitat and way of life of the herdsmen and cultivators who occupied the region. These climatic changes, however, had little effect on the evolution of the communities which succeeded each other during prehistoric times, since their progress depended mainly on the development of their own productive skills.

THE GEOGRAPHICAL ENVIRONMENT AND THE POPULATION

A distinctive feature of the present territory of Romania is the attractive variety to be seen in the landscape, with its mountains, hills, table-lands and plains. In the centre, the Transylvanian plateau lies like a citadel ringed by the walls of the Carpathian mountains; then come the Sub-Carpathians, sloping down through the hills and tablelands to the plains and the Danube valley. These regions are by no means cut off from each other, for the hills and mountain passes are easy to cross, and in the lowlands communications are facilitated by the Danube and the other rivers.

The very structure of this mountainous region offered favourable sites for human occupation in caves, on the ledges and in the valleys. Thus the hills and plains, the lake shores and the river terraces, and above all the Danube valley, all provided from the earliest times on, suitable places for settlement. The distribution of human occupation over these zones is quite clear from maps showing the diffusion of the different culture groups in prehistoric times.

These communities were able to employ the rich resources of the differing regions which supplied all the things necessary for their development. The mountains contained iron, copper, gold, silver and even tin deposits. Vineyards could flourish on the slopes and hillsides; all types of cereals spread over the fields lower down; while in many places the forest extended down to the banks of the Danube.

With the help of resources and materials taken from his natural surroundings, man succeeded, particularly after the 'Neolithic Revolution' and by the transmission of methods and inventions, in ensuring his existence by freeing himself from dependence on his environment by adapting the latter to his own requirements. The various ways of life adopted by the groups of people which succeeded one another on Romanian territory each made its contribution at successive stages of development; this meant constant improvements and growth in society from Palaeolithic times to the last phase of the Iron Age, when the Geto-Dacian civilization began to develop throughout the Carpatho-Danubian region.

Palaeolithic groups were the first to attempt to master the forces of nature and as time went on man continued to expand his skills in utilizing natural resources. From this there ultimately developed the ability to remould their surroundings on the part of those who, each in their turn, fashioned the land by their labours into the lasting human achievement it represents today.

The real history of Romania begins with the Neolithic Age, when the way of life of the people became more settled. Indeed it is only after man had gained control over the soil and certain of the natural resources, that the numerous settlements found in all parts of Romania were able to lay the foundations of a permanent population.

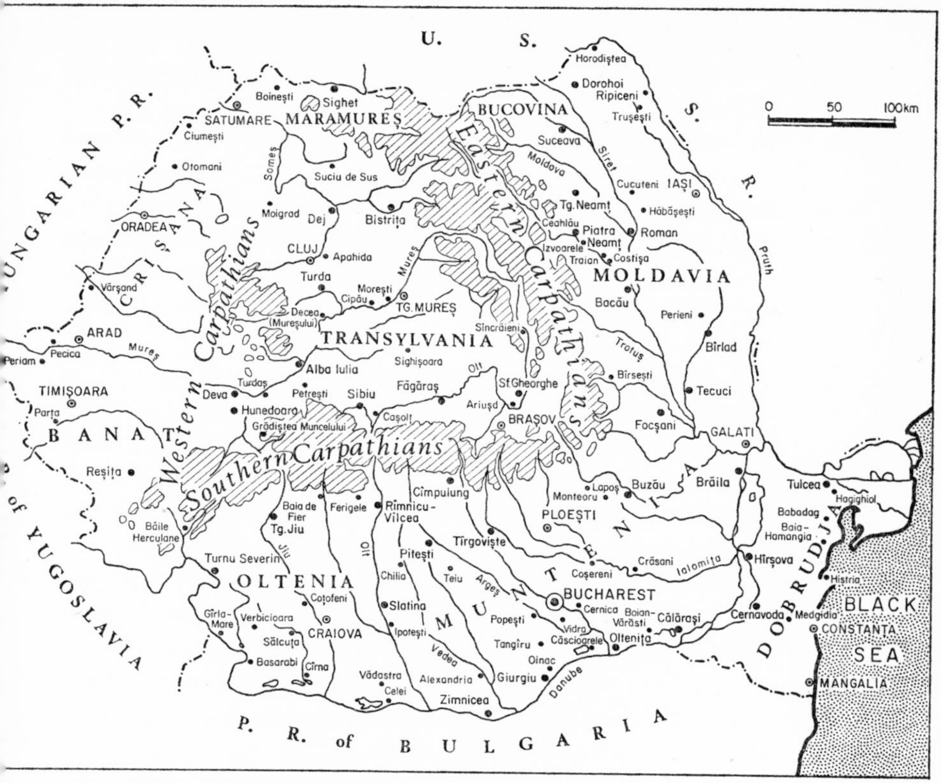

Fig. 1. Physical map of Romania, showing principal sites

In the course of several millennia this population underwent numerous and frequent modifications, and was enriched and reinforced by continuous invasions and infiltrations, from the transition period leading to the Bronze Age, when the Indo-European movements were first felt in Romania, throughout the Bronze Age when the Proto-Thracians created their magnificent cultures, until the formation of the Geto-Dacian people.

By virtue of its geographical situation and the nature of its terrain, Romania has acted as a cross-roads and been subject to continual transition; this has in turn affected its historical development. There can be no doubt that the infiltration into or penetration of Romanian territory by a succession of different cultural elements or groups, tribes or peoples made a vital contribution to the development of local cultures. In this respect attention must be drawn to the particular part played by the influences from the south, the Aegean, Anatolia and the Near East where the first civilizations, already familiar with the institution of slavery and the art of writing, had been in existence since the third millennium BC. Their effects, starting in the preceramic Neolithic, continue throughout the prehistoric and proto-historic periods. The influence of central and eastern Europe must not, however, be neglected, nor even the effect of reciprocal influences between the populations within Romanian territory itself. Their development thus fits quite naturally into the history of south-east Europe and into the history of Europe in general. *Fig. 1*

In studying the successive stages of development of these societies, account must also be taken of the distinctive aspects of the various historical provinces of Romania, such as Muntenia, Dobrudja, Moldavia, Maramureș, Crișana, Bucovina, Transylvania, Banat and Oltenia, each following slightly different trends resulting from their specific geographical conditions, but without the reciprocal links between them ever being broken. This has ensured a certain unity in the historical development of the Carpatho-Danubian region during the period which forms the subject-matter of the following chapters. It is precisely this unity of historical development, showing the essential part played by local parent stock, that recent archaeological research in Romania has so clearly revealed.

Chapter II
The Palaeolithic

THE LOWER PALAEOLITHIC

THE PEBBLE TOOL CULTURE

THE EARLIEST known tools at present existing in Romania were discovered only a few years ago along the valleys of the Dîrjov and the Dîmbovnic and other tributaries of the Olt. These are spherical pebbles, roughly chipped and shaped; the primitive technique of these tools as well as their shape and function would classify them as belonging in general to the Pebble-Tool culture, thus placing them in a very early period. But, since these pebbles were surface finds without stratigraphical context or even any evidence concerning their possible association with remains of contemporary fauna and flora, they cannot be precisely attributed to a specific geo-chronological stratum or to any definite phase of cultural evolution. However, tools of the same type as those found in Romania are known to have been widely diffused, persisting over a long period and lasting into the Middle Palaeolithic and even later. Moreover, the so-called 'Dîrjov' assemblage is heterogeneous in character since it includes, associated with these primitive tools, others of a Clactonian or Abbevillo-Acheulian type. Even this class of tools is nevertheless exceedingly primitive and rudimentary. Some of them, collected along the valleys of the Olt's tributaries are pebbles roughly shaped by flaking at one end; some are similar in form to the well-known North African spheroids. Further archaeological evidence will be necessary before a definite chronological and cultural framework can be established for these tools, which so far have only been found in a secondary context.

Recently, certain finds made at Bugiulești (Oltenia) and belonging to an upper Villafranchian horizon have been reconsidered; no adequate scientific conclusion on this subject can, however, be formulated until the results of research now in progress are known.

THE ABBEVILLIAN CULTURE

During the early Abbevillian period, contemporary with the Mindel glaciation and the Second Pluvial of the southern zone, the stone industry and the fauna tend to lose their archaic character. The distinctive tool of the Abbevillo-Chellean period is the hand-axe (*coupe de poing*), fashioned by flaking into a bifacial, generally leaf-shaped tool. In Romania, elements of this culture have also been found in the Dîrjov valley.

THE CLACTONIAN CULTURE

Even so recently as the end of the Second World War, no evidence had yet been discovered for the widely diffused and long-surviving Clactonian flake-tool industry. Now, however, there are several sites in Romania from which Clactonian tools, shaped by the 'block-on-block' technique, have been recovered; for example, those from Valea Lupului and Ripiceni. At Mitoc, in north-east Romania on the right bank of the Prut, a hearth associated with Clactonian flints has been identified. In other European and African regions, an Acheulo-Clactonian industry has been found linked to the evolution of *Pithecanthropus*. The Clactonian developed simultaneously with the Abbevillian and Acheulian industries, as can be seen from the morphological and technical features of both series of tools.

THE ACHEULIAN CULTURE

In Romania the Acheulian culture is attested by the hand-axe from Lăpușul Mic, near Cluj. Other bifacial Acheulian tools, which for a long time have been assigned to the Abbevillian, have been found during the past ten years in the Dîrjov valley.

THE LEVALLOISIAN CULTURE

The Levalloisian flake-culture is widespread in the area around Bucharest, in the Danube valley, in Moldavia, etc. A prolonged occupation attributable to this phase has been identified, on the lower terrace of the Prut, at Ripiceni, where extensive excavations carried out from 1961 to 1964 have resulted in the defining of several horizons, some persisting even during the Middle Palaeolithic period.

THE MIDDLE PALAEOLITHIC

THE MOUSTERIAN CULTURE

The Middle Palaeolithic is a transition phase both from the anthropogenetic point of view and from that of social organization. It is characterized by the Mousterian culture, which has afforded abundant archaeological evidence. Osteological remains belonging to Neanderthal man were recovered from the Ohaba Ponor cave, where three human phalanges were identified. There are abundant remains of habitation in this cave; a double hearth was found with high raised edges as well as distinctive tools such as the Mousterian points and scrapers. The burin also makes it first appearance. Tools still show the Levalloisian influence so that in Romania also it is justifiable to speak of a Levalloiso-Mousterian culture. A prolonged occupation of this type is attested at Mitoc. In Romania two main variants of points are currently found, namely, the triangular point, like the example from Baia de Fier, which recalls the Afro-microsiatic type; and the variant in the form of a large flake, like that from Ohaba Ponor resembling the west European points. Recent excavations at the 'Izvor' site of Ripiceni have revealed several Mousterian hearths. At Holboca (Moldavia) abundant remains of *Elephas primigenius* were recovered, including a skull and a tusk; its remains have also been found at Ripiceni and on river terraces in the hill region, as well as in the gravels and sands of the Danube and Tisa plains.

In addition to the Baia de Fier and Ohaba Ponor caves mentioned above, the Mousterians left habitation deposits in other caves, such as the Cheia cave (at 'Izvor') and the 'La Adam' cave (at Tîrgușor), both in Dobrudja, the Cheile Turzii, the Nandru and the Federiu caves in Transylvania, and the Carașova cave in Banat. In the Cheia and Tîrgușor caves remains were found of, among others, *Rangifer tarandus* L., *Ursus spelaeus, Hyena spelaea, Rhinoceros antiquus,* and *Equus caballus fossilis.* A similar typically cold climate fauna has also been identified in other Mousterian sites.

The Mousterian culture covers the entire territory of Romania like a blanket but within this, certain distinctive features begin to show and these persist well beyond the limits of the Mousterian phases.

THE UPPER PALAEOLITHIC

THE AURIGNACIAN CULTURE

It has for some time been accepted that in central and south-east Europe there is a strong relationship both technically and morphologically between the Mousterian and the Aurignacian cultures. Certain Aurignacian tools, from the Cioclovina cave for example, were worked with Mousterian techniques. Moreover the early Aurignacian tools show Clactonian and Szeletian influences which had been handed down through Mousterian cultures; these are attested by the foliated points from Moldavia, Transylvania, Banat, and elsewhere. As it had done during the Middle Palaeolithic period, Romanian territory continued to form an integral part of the vast Upper Palaeolithic zone covering east-central and south-east Europe. There is now abundant archaeological evidence for an Aurignacian culture in Romania; this comes partly from caves and partly from open-air sites (Mitoc, Vădastra, Iozășel, Baia de Fier, Ceahlău, etc.). Workshops for making flint tools have also been found. A site containing a deep habitation deposit has been identified on a terrace of the Bistrița, at Bistricioara (in the district of Piatra-Neamț), where research was carried out in 1957–1958. Six occupation layers belonging to Aurignacian and Gravettian culture groups have been determined. At Boinești, in Maramureș, a middle Aurignacian layer was revealed overlying a late Mousterian stratum and beneath a Gravettian level. Both the Aurignacian and Gravettian horizons contained obsidian tools. The Aurignacian as well as the Gravettian assemblages of north-west Romania quite naturally belong to the corresponding central European cultural zone,

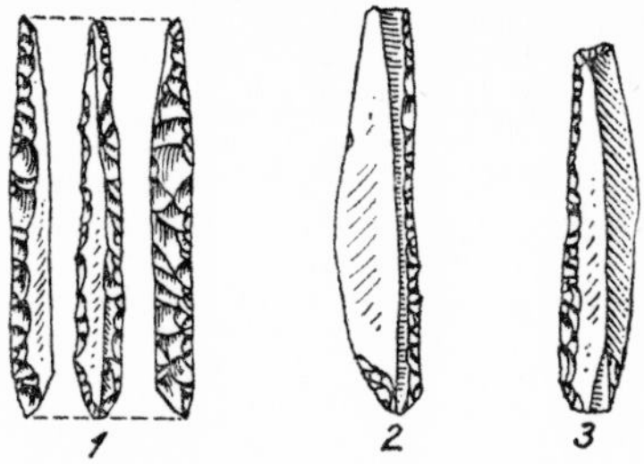

Fig. 2. Gravettian artifacts, Ceahlău. Length of 1, 3cm., others to scale

more especially with reference to Hungary and Czechoslovakia. On the eastern side of Romania, in Dobrudja, research has brought to light an Aurignacian culture which covered the entire province from the Black Sea to the Danube. Although the exact duration of this phase has not yet been clearly defined, in Dobrudja it has been possible to distinguish a late and final Aurignacian phase showing Gravettian tendencies, with affinities particularly in the Balkans, Greece and Asia Minor.

Mention must be made of the discovery in the 'La Adam' cave (Tîrguşor) of a cusp of a human tooth belonging to *Homo sapiens fossilis*. In 1942, at the Cioclovina cave (Transylvania), also in an Aurignacian layer, a neuro-cranium was found belonging to the same human type, similar to the Předmost series.

THE GRAVETTIAN CULTURE

Romanian territory, especially in the east, was once inhabited by groups of people bringing the Gravettian culture which was widespread throughout eastern Europe. These people hunted mammoth and later, although to a lesser extent, reindeer. The gradual introduction of microlithic tools, already apparent in the previous period, becomes generalized, and Gravettian microliths continue to exist until they are gradually transformed by the Mesolithic culture. Geometric flints, such as the trapeze, make their appearance. The industry, in general, consists of points of a 'La Gravette' type, blunt-back blades, scrapers, burins, microburins and shouldered points. Tools and weapons made from the bones of *Bos primigenius* or *Rangifer tarandus* have been found, for example at the site of Buda, in the Bacău

Fig. 2

region. Obsidian was widely used at this time and continued to be employed during the Mesolithic, the proto-Neolithic and the Early Neolithic periods. New environmental conditions created by a radical transformation of climate led to changes in the flora and the fauna as well as in the material equipment which now included an increasing number of microlithic tools suitable for hunting small game. In some regions subterranean dwellings with several hearths have been found belonging to small groups of Romanian Upper Palaeolithic people. Evidence has also been found of magical practices.

In the Bistriţa valley four Gravettian phases have been determined. The Gravettian element formed one of the constituents of the Pontic pre-Neolithic (or Neolithic-influenced) Tardenoisian, when the groups of hunters at a late and final stage of the surviving Upper Palaeolithic period may have been contemporary with the Mesolithic folk. From the Crimea to the Carpathians, a complete horizon with Tardenoisian trapezes was to replace or penetrate the final Gravettian level or to become intermingled with it. Relations with the Mediterranean area do not, in fact, diminish at this time. An influence which had obviously come from the Mediterranean was identified in 1954, in the Upper Palaeolithic deposits at Kostenki, where a human skeleton, with the distinctive traits of the Grimaldi type, was found. Mediterranean influences, and particularly those from Asia Minor and the Aegeo-Mediterranean zone, become intensified on the eve of the period when the food-gathering economy is gradually replaced by food-production.

Chapter III

The Mesolithic

TOWARDS A NEW STAGE IN PRIMITIVE SOCIETY

THE TRANSITION PERIOD from the Palaeolithic to the Neolithic was a time of far-reaching transformations in all fields of both material and spiritual life, for the groups of people who, ten thousand years ago, inhabited what is now Romanian territory. Although few in number, Mesolithic finds so far identified in Romania, together with the attested existence within the structure of Neolithic cultures of many microlithic-mesolithic elements, show that there was no break in continuity between the Palaeolithic and Neolithic; they also imply that the transition from one period to the other should not be over-simplified. Some communities enjoyed better living conditions than others, as for example those in the Dobrudja and at the mouths of the Danube.

THE AZILIANS

The earliest Mesolithic culture in Romania can be attributed to the Azilian people – the rather undistinguished successors of the Magdalenians, who in this area, as well as in the Caucasus and the Crimea, and on the Pontic shores in general, showed several distinctive features. A similar Azilian aspect appears in part of the archaeological material from the Băile Herculane cave, near the Iron Gates, which also contained a preceramic Neolithic horizon. In addition three small hearths, similar to those in other European sites, were found. Equipment is of a microlithic type. The distinctive tool is the crescentic blunt-back knife-blade. Micro-blades, scrapers, burins and various microlithic flakes, amongst other implements, were also recovered. Tools are not geometric in form. In general the finds in this cave show analogies with material from Montenegro and the Crimea.

THE SWIDERIAN

On the Ceahlău massif, in the east Carpathians, a Swiderian encampment has been identified at a place called 'La Scaune', at an altitude of 1327 metres. The presence of these groups of hunters in the Ceahlău mountains can probably be explained by the penetration of certain bearers of this Polish culture coming from the Desna and its tributaries, and moving south in the direction of the Black Sea and the steppes. The trial trench cut here in 1957 brought to light a large number of flints, cores, complete and broken blades some trimmed and some untrimmed and some of the so-called blunt-back type, scrapers, burins, barbed arrowheads, fragments of cores, etc. The cores are prismatic or belong to the type with an oblique striking-surface. Tools were made on the spot; they are found in different stages of manufacture. The diffusion of Swiderian cultures can therefore be assumed to extend southwards, to an area further away from the previously known centres. In addition, the Ceahlău-Scaune site, owing to its very high altitude, represents an encampment quite different in type from those already known. Its archaeological material is of a characteristically Swiderian type.

Fig. 3

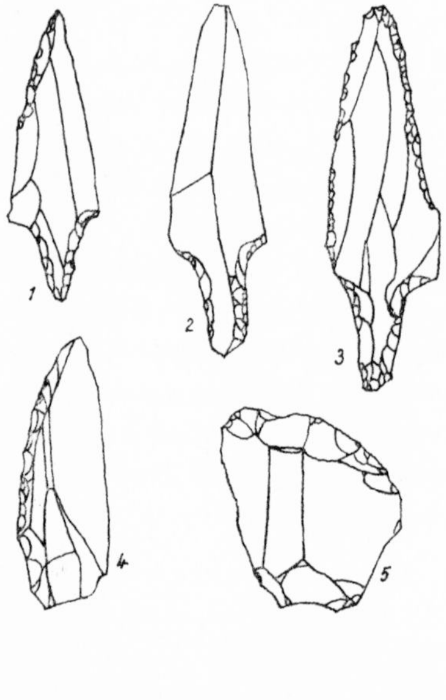

Fig. 3. Swiderian flint tools from Ceahlău-Scaune. Tanged arrowheads (1–3); blunted-back blade (4); scraper (5). Length of 1, 3.2cm., others to scale

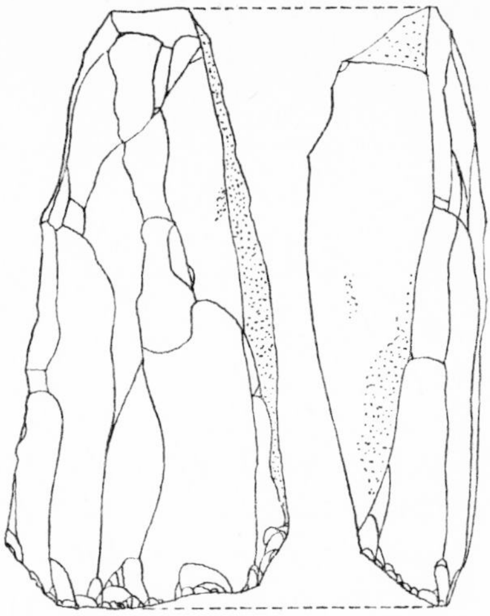

Fig. 4. Core-shaped 'push-plane', Lapoş; Neolithic Campignian. Length, 8.5cm.

The Mesolithic stage has also been identified in other Romanian sites. On the Ceahlău itself, at a place called Dîrţu, there is a Mesolithic horizon characterized by a well-documented microlithic industry showing the transition from the Gravettian to the Mesolithic. In Dobrudja at the 'La Adam' cave, finds were made in the first post-glacial archaeological level of a microlithic-Mesolithic industry; there were microlithic blades, scrapers, burins and cores, etc. This industry shows a generic continuity with the underlying final Palaeolithic horizon and is at the base of the subsequent preceramic layer. The stone material of these two levels in general shows affinities with the Mediterranean area, while certain of its features can be found in the Hamangia culture of Dobrudja.

CAMPIGNIAN AND PRE-NEOLITHIC TARDENOISIAN

Fig. 4

Archaeological excavations carried out during 1959 and 1960 at Lapoş, in the Mizil district of Ploieşti, and research undertaken at Piatra Neamţ, in Moldavia, have revealed the existence of a Campignian horizon. At Lapoş, one of the two levels yielded typically Campignian tools such as primitively made axe-blades, while in the overlying level a Neolithic-type Campignian industry was identified. Furthermore, the more

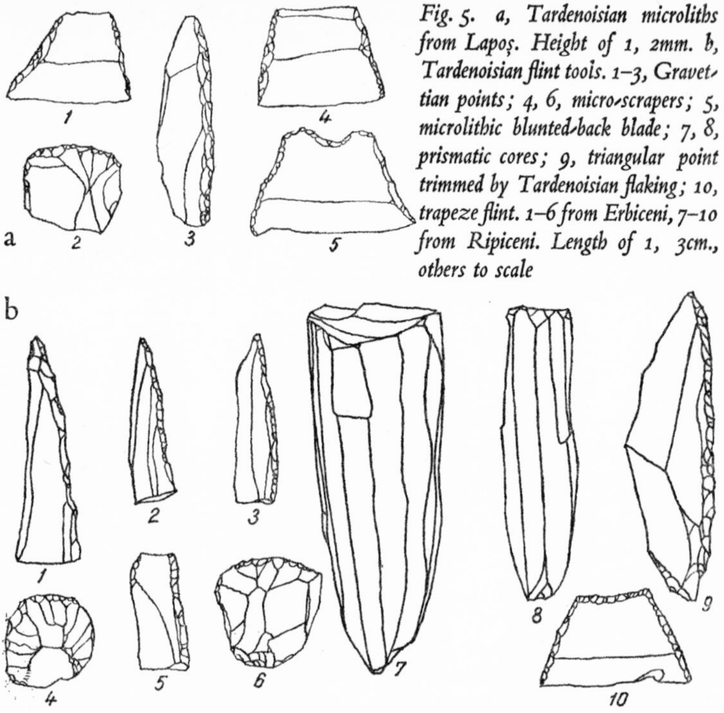

Fig. 5. a, Tardenoisian microliths from Lapoş. Height of 1, 2mm. b, Tardenoisian flint tools. 1–3, Gravettian points; 4, 6, micro-scrapers; 5, microlithic blunted-back blade; 7, 8, prismatic cores; 9, triangular point trimmed by Tardenoisian flaking; 10, trapeze flint. 1–6 from Erbiceni, 7–10 from Ripiceni. Length of 1, 3cm., others to scale

evolved microlithic-Mesolithic is documented by Tardenoisian material discovered in various parts of Romania, as for instance at Ciumeşti (Maramureş) and in the north-west at Ripiceni and Erbiceni (Moldavia) where an abundant microlithic industry was found. In addition, Tardenoisian elements are found amongst the earliest Neolithic material and even that of the two first Neolithic phases. From both the technical and morphological points of view Romanian Tardenoisian has two aspects, linking it, on the one hand, to eastern areas and on the other to east-central Europe. There is also a continuous relationship between the microlithic stratum of the Mesolithic in this region with that found in southern areas. It follows that *Fig. 5* the series of microliths and geometric flints should also be related to those in the west Pontic zone. At the end of the

Mesolithic period, in the Carpatho-Danubian area there existed an extremely heterogeneous cultural stock, and no broad cultural synthesis or even smaller cultural groups having yet been formed; this would seem to indicate the complexity of living conditions at this time. This heterogeneous stock provided the basis and the setting for the Neolithic in these regions of Europe, where various new influences were already at work.

CHAPTER IV

The Neolithic

THE ACERAMIC HORIZON

THE FIRST FARMERS AND STOCK BREEDERS

IT WAS AGAINST this background and from its elements that the Neolithic was to develop, an epoch when man moved on into a new stage of advancement during which he learned to produce for himself the means of subsistence. In Romania, the problem of the transition to the Neolithic way of life must be related to the general phenomenon which was to result in the birth and spread of Neolithic cultures in south-east and central Europe. The new way of life could not have been simultaneously introduced over so vast an area nor could it have developed everywhere at the same rate. The environment of the Near East was favourable to the establishment of the first communities whose economy was based on farming and stock-raising. Since the discoveries of 1965, in Thessaly where an aceramic horizon was revealed, new possibilities for archaeological research have been opened in other parts of south-east Europe.

Before 1959 a similar horizon was also found in the south-west U.S.S.R., at Kamena Mogila in the Ukraine. For some years it has been supposed that such levels existed in Romania, but it was not until 1962 that open-air sites were discovered with a cultural phase showing clearly the existence of an aceramic horizon. The first such site to be discovered was in an area of sand-dunes at Berea, near Ciumești in the Maramureș region, and certain other finds of this period were brought to light at Erbiceni, in the Jassy region in central Moldavia. To these sites can now be added the finds from the 'La Adam' cave in Dobrudja. These places form a triangle covering most of the territory of Romania which, however, remains open in the south-west to the penetration of preceramic Neolithic influences from Greece and the Adriatic Sea. The Berea-Ciumeşti site indicates the presence, in the Someş plain, of a centre of a proto-agricultural type of culture closely linked to that of Erbiceni and Ripiceni. All three places are on the line along which the 'Neolithic Revolution' spread to the Carpathians and hence to central Europe, from the Crimea and the north and west shores of the Black Sea. First we shall consider the Dobrudja area. The idea that a centre already practising the domestication of certain animals should have existed in the region between the Danube and the Black Sea becomes more clearly a proven fact since the new discoveries made in the 'La Adam' cave.

The aceramic horizon in Romania is documented by quite a rich series of finds of microlithic flint and obsidian tools, a large number of complete and broken blades, mostly untrimmed, blunt-back blades, notched blades, end-borers, scrapers, burins and various geometric tools in the shape of trapezes and scalene triangles; at Ciumeşti typical crescents were collected; a considerable number of microlithic flakes were also found, as well as prismatic and pyramidal cores. The black obsidian used in the Berea group of finds comes from the Carpathian region. Obsidian is plentiful also during the Early Neolithic in Romania, Hungary and Yugoslavia. The sites at Berea-Ciumeşti and Erbiceni have afforded bones of wild mammals as well as some remains of domestic animals, such as *Ovis aries L.*, *Capra* (*sive ovis*) and *Bos taurus L.* The structure and morphology of the microlithic tools remain traditionally Gravettian, a fact already observed for the Tardenoisian in Hungary. It has been possible from the 'La Adam' cave to establish a stratigraphical sequence of cultural levels, since the vertical section at this site included a complete series of horizons from the Mousterian to the Middle Neolithic, that is, the Hamangia culture. The aceramic Neolithic horizon contained an industry still technically and morphologically of a micro-Mesolithic type; there were blades, triangular barbed arrowheads, borers, burins, micro-blades, scrapers with a semi-circular working edge, flakes, etc.; some of these tools – as has already been revealed by archaeologists at the site of Tîrgușor – were evidently becoming more Neolithic in type. Research has also confirmed the complete generic continuity between the stone industry of the aceramic horizon in the deposit of this cave and that of the Hamangia culture with pottery in the same deposit. Elsewhere the stratigraphy of other Hamangia settlements has revealed the persistence of tools of a micro-Mesolithic tradition in levels of quite an evolved phase of this culture, obviously associated with other typically Neolithic tools. In this aceramic level at Tîrgușor, in addition to a few bones of wolf and hare, other bones included a fragment of skull of *Ovis aries*. Goats, however, remains of which have been found in the Hamangia levels, are lacking in the horizon in question. It has been suggested that sheep were domesticated in this area at an early phase of the aceramic Neolithic, which would imply that Dobrudja was one of the centres for the domestication of this animal.

It could be related to that in the Crimea, which in turn was linked to the preceramic centres in Iraq and Asia Minor. *Fig. 6* Certainly the microlithic industry shows striking analogies with that of the Crimea (Murzak-Koba horizon) and through this also with the centre in Iraq. But although the existence of a similar zone to the north and west of the Black Sea – part of the vast area over which the development of the Neolithic took place – cannot be doubted, this calls for more definite confirmation. The aceramic Neolithic horizon of south-east, east and north-west Romania is more closely related to this Pontic area than to the central and west Balkans. The existence of an aceramic horizon has also been reported, although as yet unconfirmed, in other parts of Romania.

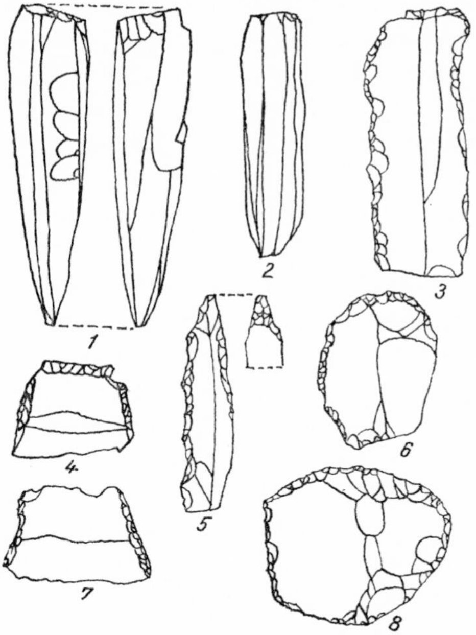

Fig. 6. Early Neolithic artifacts. Fusiform cores (1,2); flint and obsidian microliths (3–8). 1, Hamangia culture (Tîrguşor); 2, Glăvăneştii Vechi; 3–5, 7, Ciumeşti-Berea, Linear pottery culture; 6, 8, Drăghiceanu, Dudeşti culture. Length of 1, 4.2cm., others to scale

Chronologically the Romanian aceramic horizon can be dated to the sixth millennium BC, and its beginnings may have been even earlier.

THE EARLY NEOLITHIC: 5500–3500 BC

ORIGINS AND BEGINNINGS

At the end of the preceding period all south-east Europe was moving towards a Neolithic way of life. Once again, the early Romanian pottery-making Neolithic cultures cannot be separated from those of the Near East and the rest of south-east Europe. New cultures have been brought to light which cover the period stretching from the Early Neolithic to the Middle Neolithic, the Boian and the Vădastra cultures no longer representing 'the earliest Neolithic'. The history of the Neolithic first begins in the Pontic zone, closely linked to the east part

Fig. 7

of the Balkan range and to the north-west coast of the Black Sea. The climate of this region, as well as the possibility of establishing contacts with other groups of people living along the coast of the Black Sea and inland, provided better conditions for development than those prevailing in other parts of the country. The forests at that time extended down to the coasts and provided the necessary hunting ground for game to supplement food supplies and the fertile soil made cereal cultivation possible. The Pontic zone played an essential part during all the Neolithic phases and it is in this zone – to which should be added the neighbouring Danubian region – that original and distinctive cultures appeared one after the other within the unified Carpatho-Danubian setting. The earliest Neolithic in this zone was to show traces of general Mediterranean influence, which were very strongly marked at the beginning of the period. However, owing to the individual nature of the local strata and substrata and the variety of the influences affecting the Pontic zone and the Danubian area, this group gradually assumed its own structural character during the course of its development.

THE CARDIAL WARE HORIZON IN THE LOWER DANUBE

This phase arrived with the Hamangia culture which was diffused throughout Dobrudja; and it is not impossible that at a later date certain groups of people crossed to the left of the Danube to south-east Muntenia, southern Moldavia, the south of the Moldavian S.S.R., and even further along the coast to the south-west of the Ukraine S.S.R. Such a distribution is implied by the few Hamangian elements or influences that have been found. Furthermore, the analogies between the culture of the Lower Bug and that of Hamangia can only be explained if there has been actual contact between the bearers of these cultures. There is evidence of this culture also in Bulgaria, near the town of Varna and farther to the south near Burgas. Both these points represent stages on a route of penetration coming from the south, along the west coast of the Black Sea

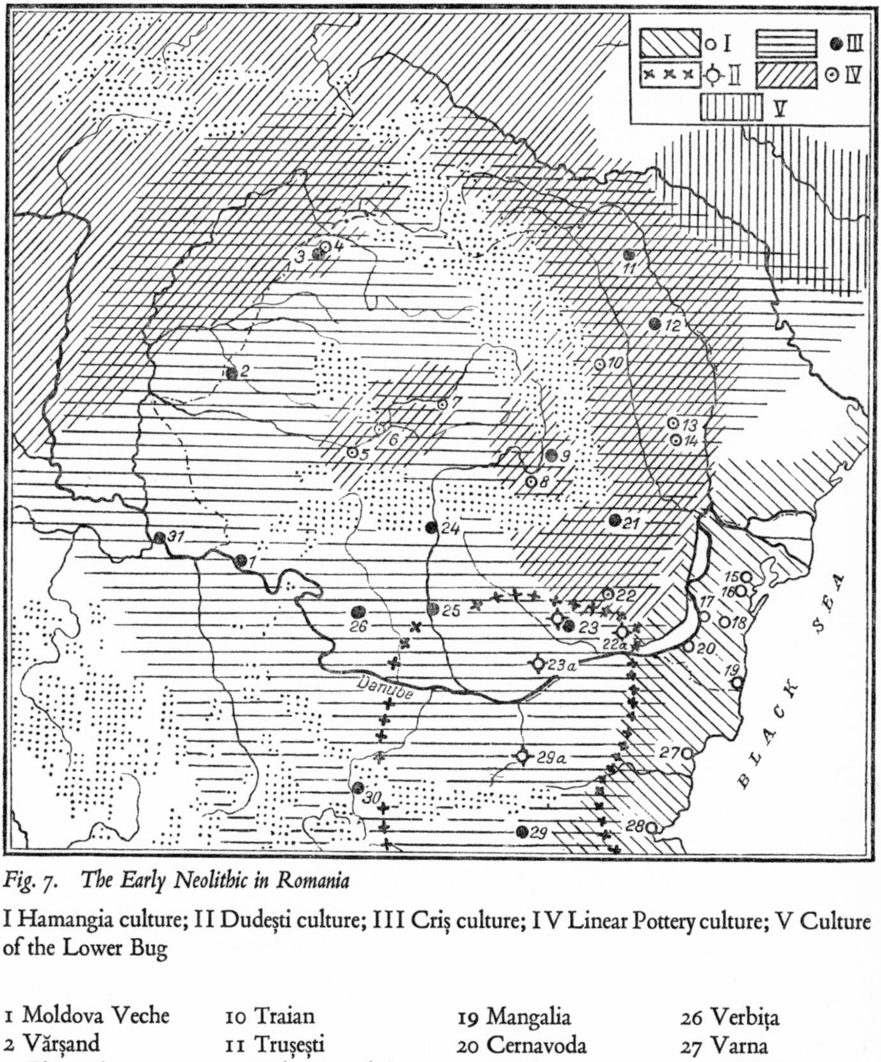

Fig. 7. The Early Neolithic in Romania

I Hamangia culture; II Dudești culture; III Criș culture; IV Linear Pottery culture; V Culture of the Lower Bug

1 Moldova Veche
2 Vărșand
3 Ciumești
4 Berea (Ciumești)
5 Turdaș
6 Alba Iulia
7 Cipău
8 Hărman
9 Leț
10 Traian
11 Trușești
12 Valea Lupului
13 Perieni
14 Sălceni
15 Ceamurlia de Jos
16 Baia (Hamangia)
17 Capidava
18 Gura Dobrogei
19 Mangalia
20 Cernavoda
21 Băești
22 Coșereni
22a Boian (Vărăști)
23 Bucharest
23a Drăghiceanu
24 Valea Răii
25 Cireașov
26 Verbița
27 Varna
28 Kableșkovo
29 Karanovo
29a Hotnița
30 Kremikovci
31 Starčevo

towards the mouth of the Danube. A similar culture has been identified in Thessaly, at Montenegro, in Dalmatia, northern and southern Italy, Sicily, southern France, Spain and on the coast of Portugal and North Africa. It would appear that this horizon which spread around the Mediterranean originated in Cilicia and Syria. It was from here that the first Neolithic navigators set sail, making use of the shores and islands. At a later phase they penetrated into the hinterland, as, for instance, in Dobrudja and Thessaly. It is feasible that other regions, such as North Africa where a primitive realistic art similar to the Hamangian has been found recently, formed part of this general movement around the Mediterranean. The arrival by sea of the first Neolithic pottery-users in the south-east of Romania – the Danubian-Pontic area – in small boats hollowed from a single log is indicated, not only by similar finds of pottery decorated with impressions of a *cardium* shell – hence the name of 'Cardial Pottery' or 'Cardial Ware' horizon – but also by the deep-sea fishing known to have been practised by the Hamangian
Plate 1 people. Excavations in Dobrudja have, in fact, yielded the bones of large species of fish, such as the *Aurata aurata,* which live far from the shore. The precise date when people of the Cardial Ware horizon first settled in Romania is difficult to determine with certainly, but scientific evidence confirms that it was they who created or spread the earliest Neolithic pottery culture. At the time of their arrival the climate of Dobrudja
Plate 2 was of the steppe type as testified by the remains of *Equus (Asinus) hydruntinus Reg.,* which most probably originated in the steppes of Asia. This species was widespread in Europe during the Upper Pleistocene but later disappeared. Its reappearance (during the Holocene) in Europe and Cyrenaica (where it has been reported during the last few years) can only be explained by a return to climatic conditions of the steppe. Outside the zone of the Hamangia culture, this species has also been identified in the area of the Starčevo-Criș culture, which is in part

contemporary with the former. No doubt the new arrivals found, in the Pontic region, a local preceramic substratum which has absorbed the Neolithic elements.

THE NORTH PONTIC AND BUG AREAS

The discovery of Early and Middle Neolithic remains in Romania and the south-west of the Soviet Union has also suggested that there may have been certain cultures that developed in parallel and only later came into contact and influenced one another. Similar contacts may have been established between the Hamangia group which was extending towards the north and north-east and the Lower Bug culture spreading south and south-westwards. Pottery of the Bug culture, by its technique, forms and decoration, shows affinities with that of the Hamangia culture; other features reflect general Mediterranean influences. The two cultures also resemble one another in their microlithic implements and they exercised a common influence although from different directions; their combined results are to be seen, however, in the Cucuteni-Tripolje painted ware assemblage.

One of the centres, therefore, from which the Neolithic gradually developed and spread in Romania is precisely this Danubian-Pontic area, closely linked to the zone north of the Black Sea, the Lower Bug and Asia Minor.

NEOLITHIC-INFLUENCED CAMPIGNIAN

Recent discoveries and observations, such as those at Lapoș, in the wooded hills of north-east Muntenia on a tributary of the Buzău, made in 1959–1960 and 1962–1963, show that already Neolithic-influenced Campignian, with typical macrolithic tools, existed there. The upper level at Lapoș was characterized by the form and technique of the macrolithic tools and the material employed, as well as by several sherds of very primitively made pottery. This same stratigraphical horizon also contained microliths attributable to a Neolithic-influenced Tardenoisian. Archaeological evidence from Muntenia, Moldavia, Maramureș, Transylvania and Banat confirms the existence of a wide Campignian front which can be related to the development and advance of Campignian people coming from the south, as well as to the speeding-up of the transition to Neolithic life. The southern origin of Campignian, its derivation over a wide area from Palaeolithic cultures, as well as the continuance of macrolithic elements in Late Neolithic cultures in Romania and the south-west of the U.S.S.R., all go to show that the finds belonging to the Campignian horizon in the Carpatho-Danubian area form an integral part of the general historical picture of Europe, Africa and the Near East. There can therefore be no doubt whatever that the Campignian population was not only a persistent and extremely active element in the Romanian Neolithic, but also one of the forces behind the transition from a hunting and gathering economy (food-gatherers) to one of cultivators and stock-breeders (food-producers). In the light of this fact, the southern origin of Campignian appears even more probable when it is considered that the tool termed a *pick* implies from the functional point of view that the bearers of this culture tilled the soil.

THE NEOLITHIC-INFLUENCED TARDENOISIAN

The Tardenoisian element showed itself to be as strong as, and even stronger than, those of Campignian origin, both influences being seen together in some areas. Tardenoisian sites are found in the open country. Recent excavations at Ciumeşti, Erbiceni and Ripiceni have yielded a rich microlithic inventory: numerous blades and micro-blades, end-scrapers and flakes, in the form of microlithic points, geometric flints such as triangles, trapezes and crescents; burins and cores, some of which are prismatic, and so on. In addition to flint, obsidian from the Carpathians was also used. Studies of material from a chronologically and culturally Tardenoisian horizon found in Moldavia, as well as in Maramureş, indicate that stock-breeding may have been practised at this time. The analogies which exist between the Tardenoisian in Romania (types and variants of scrapers made from round or oval flakes, trapezes, fusiform cores, etc.) and that found to the north-west of the

Black Sea and in the Crimea reveal the wide extent of the cultural zone west and north-west of the Black Sea.

The archaeological material of all the early Romanian cultures includes a flint or obsidian industry of a Tardenoisian type. Tardenoisian folk assured the continuity of development, providing, with other microlithic groups, not only the framework but also the impetus towards a Neolithic way of life, which during its long and complex development absorbed all the local groups and also included other external elements.

THE PAINTED WARE HORIZON

One of the innovations introduced from the Near East was the technique of painting pottery before firing. Almost all the Romanian territory was included within the area covered by the painted pottery horizon, only the Pontic 'Cardial' region being excluded. The newly arrived groups of people also brought with them agricultural improvements in the form of new species of domestic animals and cultivated plants. They belonged to the great cultural group of the early painted-pottery Neolithic, which spread from the Near East far into the Carpathian region, and covered all south-east Europe; within this area, however, there are regions of varying sizes with distinctive characteristics. In Yugoslavia, similar elements form the Starčevo culture which extends into south-west Romania (Banat, Oltenia), in north-west Bulgaria there is the Kremikovci group, while in south Bulgaria the Karanovo (painted-ware horizon) was developing at this time. In western Romania, Moldavia and in eastern Hungary the Criș culture is found. This culture expanded eastwards as far as the Bug valley where it came into contact with the Bug culture. In Greece the proto-Sesklo cultures were just beginning.

The development of the Criș phase in Romania lasted longer than the Starčevo facies and it seems to have been preceded – at least in the zones open to the Black Sea – by certain local cultures. The Neolithic pottery-bearers did not therefore penetrate into an empty wasteland. Settlements were situated

near streams, on the lower river terraces or in the immediate neighbourhood of watercourses; material from habitation sites has also been found in caves. There is no evidence of any fortified sites. Settlements appear to be of a dispersed type, the semi-subterranean dwellings or surface huts being at some distance from each other. At Glăvăneştii Vechi, however, six surface dwellings were found grouped together. Most of the huts are rectangular; some subterranean dwellings have an entrance stairway and are divided into two rooms. The most
Plate 17 important sites are those at Leţ, near Sf. Gheorghe, where the Criş horizon includes three levels, and at Perieni, in Moldavia, where for the first time the stratigraphical and chronological position of the Criş culture in relation to the Linear Pottery culture was established; it is the latter which overlies the former. Other sites where systematic excavations have been carried out are to be found to the south of the Carpathians, in Oltenia; there is one at Valea Răii, near Rîmnicu-Vîlcea, with two cultural levels, and another at Verbiţa, in the zone of intersection of the plain and the Getic ridge, where the archaeological deposit also contains two levels. Flint tools, such as blades, scrapers, points and trapezes, are of a microlithic type; there
Plate 8 are also microlithic cores and sickle-flints for curved horn handles. The only sickle of this type as yet found in the area covered by the Starčevo-Criş culture was unearthed at Valea Răii, in 1963; it lay in a large storage jar located in the corner of a hut. Several flints were still mounted in a slot cut in the curved handle. This sickle is similar to the Karanovo type in Bulgaria and to the Natufian and Haçılar type from the Near
Fig. 8 East. As well as flint, locally worked obsidian was employed. Polished stone axes were flat or trapeze-shaped; and there are
Plate 7 also 'shoe last' axes; at Valea Răii I discovered a very small axe. There were characteristic bone spatulae as well as chisels, awls and borers, and similar tools of bone. The typical spindle-whorls of baked clay have four arms but there are other bi-

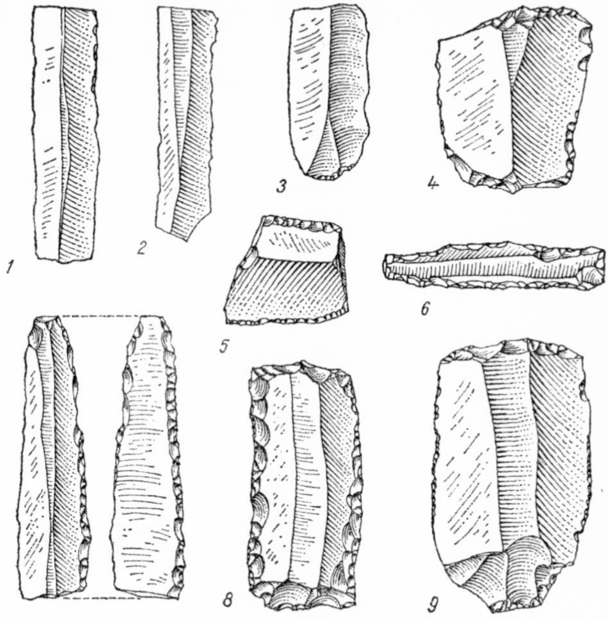

Fig. 8. Obsidian (3) and flint (1, 2, 4–9) microliths of the Criș culture from Valea Răii (Oltenia). 1–4, level I; 5–9, Level II, Length of 1, 3.3cm.

conical or conical examples. Loom-weights have also been recovered. Pottery includes the three following main groups: (a) Coarse, chaff-tempered ware, often undecorated; (b) fine burnished slipped ware; and (c) painted ware, which might be monochrome, bichrome or even trichrome. The decorative motifs are black or occasionally white on a red ground and consist of narrow or wider parallel lines, or of hatched triangles; *Fig. 9* spirals are less frequent. Incised decorations in corn husk or honeycomb designs and decorations made by the impression of a shell of the fresh-water oyster also occur.

Pottery is very varied in form. The most characteristic vase is the large globular, long-necked jar used for storing food and water; also to be found are 'barrel' vases and vases on a high pedestal of a cruciform, round or square section. Certain of the profiles as well as the primitive channelling, which appears for

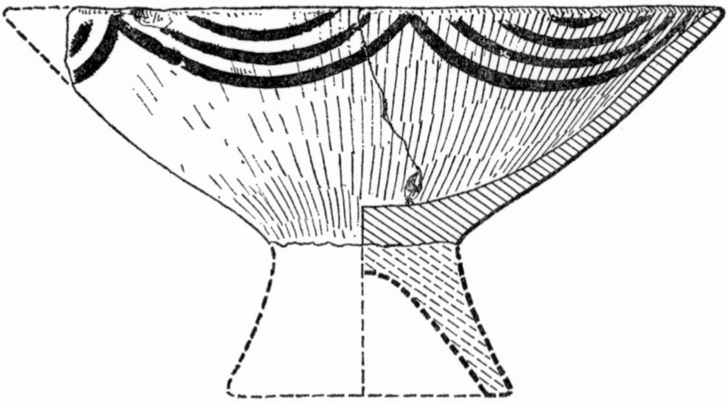

Fig. 9. Pedestalled bowl with painted decoration from Valea Răii, Criș culture. Height of bowl from reconstructed base, 6.6cm.

the first time, announce the coming of the Vinča culture, the roots of which can be partly found in the Starčevo-Criș material. Evidence of the beliefs and ritual of the period are seen in the earthenware altars and the anthropomorphic and zoomorphic clay idols; in level I at Valea Răii were two broken figurines of rams with traces of red and black paint. There were clay stamps of a southern type used for either body painting or for fabric printing. The dead were buried in a contracted position; cemeteries are unknown; at Valea Lupului (Jassy), however, a double tomb was found. From the anthropological point of view, the Starčevo-Criș folk were a heterogeneous group. Personal ornaments consisted of *Spondylus* and *Tridacna* shells obtained by inter-tribal exchanges made over a vast area. Economic activities included farming (*Triticum monococcum* was cultivated) and stock-breeding. From a hut at Verbița were recovered the remains of *Equus* (*Asinus*) *hydruntinus Reg.*, which has also been identified in the same cultural period in Hungary and Yugoslavia, as well as in Dobrudja in the zone of the Hamangia culture.

The relative chronological position of the Romanian Starčevo-Criș material has been ascertained at Leț (in south-east Transylvania), where it underlies a Boian (phase II) cultural level; at Verbicioara (in Oltenia), where it is covered by the Vinča culture; at Perieni (Moldavia), where it is associated with Linear Pottery; while in central Transylvania certain of its traits continue to develop into the Middle Neolithic. This horizon, of east Mediterranean origin, persisted a considerable time in some areas, and it contributed to the formation of the Petrești and Cucuteni cultures. Radiocarbon readings on material from Gyálarét, Katalszeg and Hódmezövásárhely Kotacpart in Hungary, as well as from Vršnik (Starčevo III phase) and Gornja Tuzla (final Starčevo phase) in Yugoslavia (5140±100 BC; 4420±100 BC; 4500±100 BC; 4915±50 BC; and 4449±75 BC, respectively) set the date of the Criș culture in general in a period prior to the Linear Pottery culture in central Europe, while the latter is itself dated to the end of the fifth millennium BC.

THE LINEAR POTTERY CULTURE

According to generally accepted opinion, various groups of people broke away from the original centre of this culture, in the loess regions of central Europe, and spread out in all directions; westwards they reached Belgium and the Paris Basin and eastwards the Basin of the Bug. The presence of these Linear Pottery people in Romania has been discovered only in the past fifteen years, their extension to the south-east being fixed by the Lower Danube. The whole of Moldavia was overrun or even settled by Linear Pottery tribes; this is equally true in Transylvania and north-east Muntenia as far as the area surrounding Bucharest. Tribes bringing the Linear Pottery culture penetrated into the Carpatho-Danubian zone by two different routes: one north of the Carpathians, whence various groups spread southward towards the mouth of the Danube and north-east Muntenia while others reached the Bug valley; the second started from Slovakia and north-east Hungary whence the respective groups penetrated along the river valleys into south-east Transylvania. The first phase, that of the north-west, is characterized by pottery decorated with deeply incised bands and lines in continuous spiral and meander designs. The distinctive form is the high-pedestalled cup, the profile and painted decoration of which was already found in the late phase of the Criș culture at Valea Răii. The culture of north-west Romania, represented principally by the Ciumești-Berea (Maramureș) material is linked to the 'East Slovakian' Linear Pottery or that of the 'Hungarian Plain' (Alföld), documented by finds from Tarnabod and other east Hungarian sites. Radio-carbon analysis of Tarnabod material gave a date of 4330 ± 100 BC, which is also applicable to the Ciumești-Berea horizon in Romania. In other zones of Romania the Linear Pottery of a 'music note' (*Notenkopf*) style is found. The stratigraphical and chronological position of this ware was established for the first time at Perieni (Moldavia), where the Linear Pottery culture level overlies the Criș occupation. In Moldavia (Traian, the site of Dealul Fîntînilor) and in the Moldavian S.S.R. (Florești) the Linear Ware horizon underlies the pre-Cucuteni horizon, and in Muntenia it is covered by a Boian I layer. In Transylvania, some sherds of 'music note' Linear Pottery ware appear in the level which terminates the Middle Neolithic evolution and precedes the Petrești culture. It would seem, therefore, that bearers of this style penetrated quite late into the Carpatho-Danubian region, while the Ciumești-Berea culture is somewhat earlier. Sites are found on the lower terraces of watercourses or even in their valleys (Glăvăneștii Vechi on the River Jijia). Semi-subterranean dwellings have been identified, as well as huts, sometimes grouped together; but large rooms, similar to those found in the original centres of these tribes, have not yet been discovered. Among the tools are the distinctive polished stone 'shoe last' adze, and the flat trapeze-shaped axe/adze, some of them quite large; these are found in dwellings

Plate 16

and deposits, as for example at Glăvăneştii Vechi. Flint and obsidian tools are markedly microlithic (trimmed and untrimmed blades, notched blades, scrapers; there are also geometric flints, the trapeze being the most frequent); flint and obsidian fusiform cores are likewise found. Pottery may be divided into two types: the first is coarse, chaff-tempered ware, decorated with rows of simple channelled grooves or with raised barbotine (honeycomb) designs. The second type includes fine ware of greyish-black fabric, vases being decorated with incised bands or 'music-note' (*Notenkopf*) motifs. The most typical shapes are hemispherical bowls and small straight-sided bowls. Some of the coarser vases intended for storing foodstuffs were decorated by rustication. The pottery shows strong affinities with that of the Criş culture, as regards technique, shapes and rusticated decoration, as well as in the decorative motifs such as the spiral or line designs, etc. In view of these resemblances it has been suggested that this pottery had its origin in the Criş culture, from which it also inherited its art. However this may be, the legacies left by the Criş and Linear Pottery cultures played a most important part in the formation of subsequent cultures such as pre-Cucuteni, Boian, Tisa and the pre-Petreşti, not to mention the zones where the influences of both factors converged. Similarly, the signs of actual contacts between the Linear Pottery and Hamangia cultures are becoming gradually more evident.

MEDITERRANEAN IMPULSES

There are indications of reciprocal influences between the Cardial Ware element, the Central European Linear Pottery culture, the painted ware of Aegeo-Mediterranean origin and the elements found in the Lower Bug culture north of the Black Sea. It is not surprising, therefore, that the Cucuteni-Tripolye painted ware first appeared in this very area where these varied elements were in contact. A further series of discoveries has centred attention on another element also of Aegeo-Mediterranean origin. In this zone where the Starčevo-Criş, Hamangia and Linear Pottery cultures met and intermingled, a new culture belonging to the Early Neolithic has been defined, showing clear affinities with the Vinča culture.

THE DUDEŞTI CULTURE *Fig. 10*

In the Bucharest region, crudely fired pottery of a rough fabric, but with a uniform highly burnished black or greyish-black slip has been discovered. The ornamentation of vases consists of parallel channels grouped either obliquely or at an angle; from the earliest occupation level the spiral appears as a decorative motif, made by placing small grooves very close together. Important is incised ware with a decoration consisting of curving lines, meanders, zig-zags or of parallel obliquely hatched bands. It was chiefly from this ware that Vădastra I pottery developed. The technically primitive ware made of chaff-tempered fabric takes the form of large vessels. The fine black or greyish-black ware, made of sand-tempered fabric includes hollow-footed cups. There are also biconical vases with small protuberances. Links with the Criș-Starčevo ware can also be seen in the very open type of biconical bowl. The shape of the large globular vases, as well as the decorative motifs, enable analogies to be drawn with discoveries made at Can Hasan in Anatolia, as also with material from Çatal Hüyük in Anatolia and the Maritza river basin, in southern Bulgaria. This pottery is sometimes associated with microliths, including conical and prismatic cores, re-touched blades, simple or double scrapers (on blades or flakes), trapezes, etc. Also among the archaeological material are small trapezoidal flat axes, various bone tools, clay spindle-whorls and zoomorphic and anthropomorphic figurines. The persistence of a Tardenoisian tradition is shown by the presence of microliths. The pottery, however, by its technique (especially the black channelled ware) as well as its forms and decorative motifs, confirms the southern Aegeo-Anatolian origin of this culture which spread across southern Bulgaria towards the Lower Danube. The starting point can be found in south-west Anatolia, whence it crossed the Aegean and southern area of Bulgaria (finds at Hotnița, near Trnovo, re-

Fig. 10. Sherds of Dudeşti ware. 1, Drăghiceanu; 2–5, Bucharest (Fundenii Doamnei)

presenting a stage in this move northwards). This culture appears to be very closely related to the Vinča, but it constitutes an earlier phase than even the beginnings of the latter. Its area of diffusion, as far as it can be determined at present, covers south-east Oltenia, north-central Bulgaria and Muntenia. It is possible that it may have also spread into south-east Transylvania and south Moldavia.

From the first excavations carried out at Dudeşti (a district of Bucharest) a non-homogeneous cultural assemblage, divided into two different levels – Dudeşti I and Dudeşti II – was identified. It is to the first of these levels only that the name of Dudeşti culture is given; the second level belongs to a different group. The Dudeşti culture, as it is defined here, is completely independent of the Vinča and Veselinovo cultures although closely related to both of them; it has close links also with the Hamangia culture and between them are to be found reciprocal influences.

THE VINČA CULTURE

In west and south-west Romania, during the early Neolithic, the Vinča culture arose and developed, and is well documented

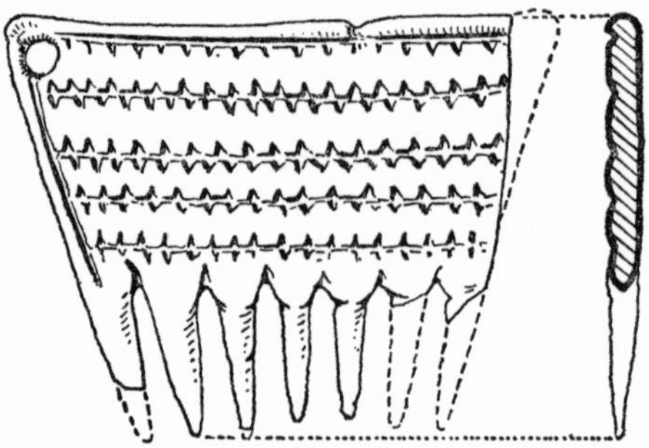

Fig. 11. Bone comb found at 'Lumea Nouă' (Alba Iulia) in 1963. Middle Neolithic. Height, 4 cm.

in Banat and west and south-west Oltenia; in Transylvania it is known as the Turdaş culture or the Turdaş facies. The reciprocal influences of the Dudeşti and Vinča cultures were very strong particularly in the zone of interpenetration, a fact which has led certain authors to extend the Vinča culture to the east of the Olt or to suppose that the Vinča folk penetrated from the mouth of the Danube towards the Iron Gates and the site of Vinča itself. The distinctive elements of this new culture were: the black pottery; a series of vessel shapes such as the hollow-pedestalled vases, and bowls; and, in particular, the decorative technique, south-eastern in origin, of small close-set fluted lines. Certain features recalling the Starčevo-Criş-Karanovo cultures, such as the channelled ware and the pedestalled cups, were to develop subsequently. Pottery painted before firing also continued to be made; in fact, as is evidenced both stratigraphically and culturally in central Transylvania, it lasted until the beginning of the Late Neolithic, when it was adopted by the bearers of the Petreşti culture. The Vinča and the Turdaş folk also used pottery richly decorated with bands outlined by incised lines and filled in with dots or lines. The stone industry still included microliths. Spindle-whorls and loom-weights were in extensive use at this time. In addition to stock-breeding some cereals, especially *Triticum vulgare*, were cultivated. In Transylvania and Banat the bearers of this culture came into

Plate 9

Plate 10

Fig. 11

Plate 18

contact with the Tisa folk, whose culture appears in a later phase at Băile Herculane, Deva and Reci. The tablets from Tărtăria, which I attribute to the last horizon of the Middle Neolithic, so resemble examples from Uruk IIIB (Mesopotamia) as to confirm the absolute chronology (2900–2700 BC) of the end of the Turdaș and the beginning of the Petrești cultures. Plate 11

THE MIDDLE NEOLITHIC: 3500–2700 BC

Towards the middle of the fourth millennium BC, the Neolithic tribes of the vast Carpatho-Danubian region had reached a stable social and economic way of life characteristic, in its essential traits, of the Neolithic in its fully-developed form. The early over-all cultural unity was broken, and in the different areas there was a tendency to form new cultures and new syntheses. The interpenetration and reciprocal action of influences originating in the Mediterranean, central Europe, and the southern Bug culture led to material and spiritual enrichment and stimulated local development, all of which contributed to progress in general. At this time there was a certain degree of biological and anthropological intermingling. Neolithic life took on a more markedly agricultural aspect, which is reflected in the more closely grouped permanent villages. Towards the end of the period, it became necessary in certain cultures to fortify sites with defensive ditches. The polishing technique gradually improved and the number of tools showing a functional differentiation of types increased. It was about the middle of this period that the use of the shaft-hole axe became widespread; the shoe-last axe was gradually replaced by the trapeze-shaped axe. A few members only of the tribe now possessed small copper objects, such as jewellery, implements and ritual objects. Microliths still occur but they are no longer a general or determining feature. At the end of the phase, the number of deer-antler adzes in use increases, also indicating a more stable life *Fig. 12* and an increase in plant cultivation. Raw materials, such as flint or *Spondylus* shells for ornaments, were obtained by wider trade connections between different tribes. Similarly at this period, new cultures grew up although in certain regions the older cultures continued their evolution.

THE HAMANGIA CULTURE

The Hamangia culture reached its climax during the Middle Neolithic but disappeared by the end of this phase. Although this culture was affected by certain influences of the Linear Pottery and Bug cultures as well as by the new influx from the south, it nevertheless retained its individuality and continued evolving throughout the Middle Neolithic. In the preceding chapter the early phase of this culture and its area of diffusion and origin were described. In the Pontic zone, during the period under discussion, several phases are discernible. The first of these was the transition phase to the Gumelniţa culture. During this period settlements are still situated on the lower terraces, near watercourses, on the hill slopes and even in caves, as at Gura Dobrogei. Sometimes the villages temporarily assume the aspect of *tells*. Dwellings are still generally detached, however, and within the same site there may be subterranean and semi-subterranean huts; larger surface structures continue to be scarce. Microliths attest the persistence of the Tardenoisian element. Nevertheless there are other larger flint tools (such as blades and side-scrapers) similar to those of the Boian culture and which are in part a survival from the final Palaeolithic era. Axes made from hard stone, such as granite and other similar material are quite frequent. The Hamangian axe with a quadrangular or bi-convex section is typologically related to those from the Aegeo-Mediterranean area and even Thessaly. The flat trapeze-shaped axe was also used although the hollow-bored axe is still unknown. Copper objects are still extremely rare and metallurgy is only at its beginnings. Awls and chisels were fashioned from bone, and deer-antlers were used in the manufacture of adzes. A series of local and regional stone tools

Plate 2

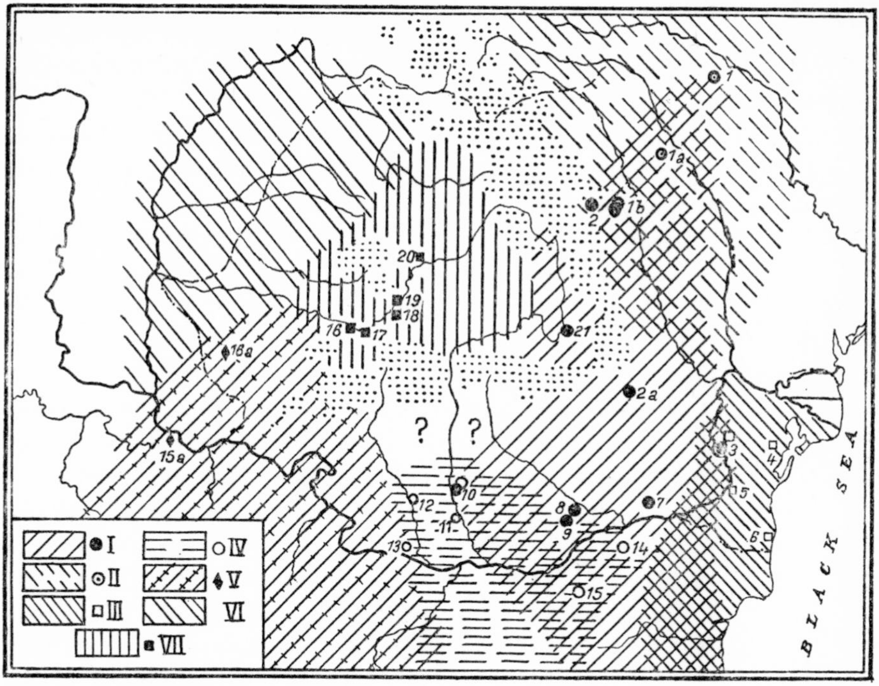

Fig. 12. The Middle Neolithic in Romania

I Boian culture; II Pre-Cucuteni culture; III Hamangia culture; IV Vădastra culture; V Vinča culture; VI Tisa II and III culture; VII Turdaş culture

1 Floreşti
1a Larga Jijiei
1b Traian/Zăneşti
2 Zăneşti
2a Aldeni
3 Hîrşova
4 Baia (Hamangia)
5 Cernavoda
6 Mangalia
7 Boian-Vărăşti
8 Tangîru
9 Petru Rareş
10 Slatina
11 Hotărani
12 Şimnicu
13 Vădastra
14 Kara-Agač
15 Čakmak-Tepe
15a Vinča
16 Tăualaş
16a Parţa
17 Turdaş
18 Tărtăria
19 Alba Iulia
20 Cheile Turzii
21 Leţ

seems to suggest a macrolithic Campignian element. Among the distinctive features of this culture are the forms, the technique, and the decoration of the pottery. The first group comprises the coarse ware tempered with crushed potsherds. The second group includes the fine and very fine ware, of better-worked fabric tempered with fine sand or carefully ground potsherds. The outer surface of the pottery is black, brown-black or greyish, and highly burnished. It assumes a great variety of forms, including large, medium and small globular amphorae sometimes provided with a hemispherical lid; cylindrical or B-profile bottles, some of which have a pedestal; pedestalled cups recalling those found in the Criș and Linear Pottery culture; 'tiered vessels' which appear in the final phases; there are also numerous decorated bowls with incurved rims. The coarse ware is rusticated; it is decorated with notched or deeply incised bands in relief, some of the designs having been impressed with a *Cardium* shell. Technically the decoration of the richly ornamented fine ware consists of incised lines, and series of dots and dotted lines; there is also incrusted and channelled ware. Decorative motifs are sometimes repeated a number of times on the vase; and metope and triglyph designs were also used. The Hamangia folk also made marble vases but

Fig. 13

Plate 1

Fig. 14

Fig. 13. a, Typical pot form from Ceamurlia de Jos; b, pedestalled bowl from Baia; Hamangia culture. Height of a, 10.2cm.; of b, 8.7cm.

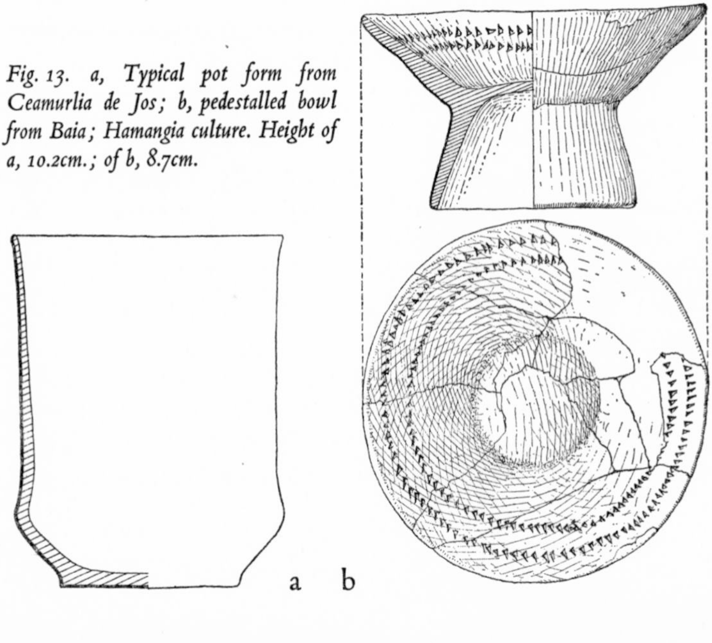

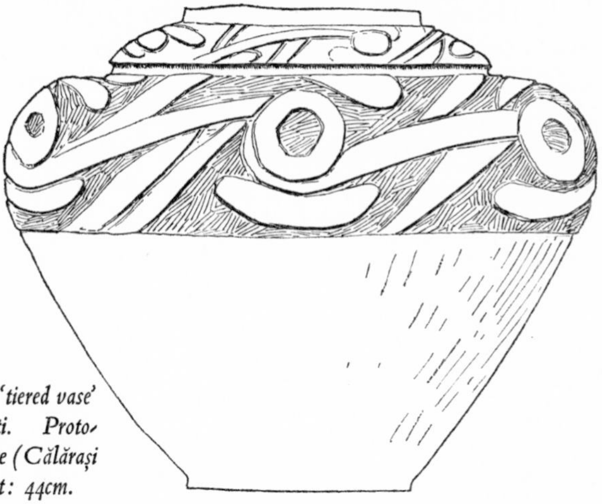

Fig. 14. Large 'tiered vase' from Ciumești. Proto-Gumelnița culture (Călărași Museum) Height: 44cm.

these were very rare. Solid but elegant marble bracelets have been found as well as cylindrical and other beads and bracelets made from such shells as *Spondylus gaederopus*. A chance find of several copper bangles was made at Agigea near Constanța; and a small bead in the same material was recovered from the Cernavoda cemetery. The presence of personal ornaments made from *Spondylus* shells obtained during the Middle Neolithic by inter-tribal exchanges confirms that the Hamangia groups formed part of the distribution zone of such ornaments, which are in fact found among all the cultures of this period in Romania and the adjoining countries; this type of jewellery spread even farther afield in central Europe.

One of the novel features of the Hamangian culture is the quite exceptionally rich art. In addition to the few marble figurines, a number of baked clay examples have been found. These latter may be divided into two types: the silhouetted standing type of figurine, and the seated type. It is usually a female figure which is represented, probably related to a fertility

Plate 6

cult. The head and neck are shown as a column without indications of eyes, nose, mouth or ears. The arms are drawn in under the well-defined breasts or rest on the stomach. The portrayal of the hips and sexual attributes is exaggerated. One figurine, of particular artistic value, found at Cernavoda, represents a man seated on a stool in the attitude of a thinker. Another, also in baked clay, from the same tomb, represents a woman sitting on the ground in a resting position. These two form the celebrated 'Cernavoda couple'. Hamangian art is remarkable for its wealth, originality and variety as well as for its archaic realism.

Plates 3–5

THE BURIAL RITE

The dead were interred in an extended position. The largest cemetery to have been excavated is that of Cernavoda, where more than 400 burials were found. Grave goods included a flat axe (almost invariably), pots, idols, marble or *Spondylus*-shell ornaments, symbolic and geometric-shaped tools as well as food-offerings. Occasionally skulls were buried either alone or in groups. The economy of the Hamangia folk was of a mixed type.

Plate 6

The Vinča culture also developed during the Middle Neolithic in south-west Oltenia and Banat. Similarly, in central Transylvania, the Turdaș aspect manages to survive by transmitting its tradition of painted ware to the Petrești culture, of which it forms one of the essential elements.

Plate 11

THE VĂDASTRA CULTURE

This culture is represented by sites in central Muntenia and north-central Bulgaria. The principal type of habitation is the semi-subterranean oval or quadrangular dwelling; but there are also huts. Tools include small polished stone axes, some of the 'shoe-last' type. Pottery decoration may be incised, or excised and filled in with white paste. Decorative motifs are clearly geometric in character; vessels of finer ware are ornamented with fluting and corrugations. The decoration has affinities with that employed by Hamangia and Veselinovo folk. The technique and forms as well as the decorations of the pottery show a south Mediterranean influence. The Vădastra I developed mainly from the Dudești culture. The 1963 excavations (Hotărani) confirm that the old denomination of 'Vădastra I' and 'Vădastra II' do not fit the facts and that channelled ware occurs – as at Boian – in all four Vădastra phases. There are signs of phase II also south of the Danube – where it is contemporary with Boian Ib, Ic, and IIa. Phase III, representing the classical period of this culture, corresponds to Boian IIb and IIc. A fourth phase, identified at Slatina, is contemporary with the Boian III phase. Finally, during the Boian V, both cultures merge. Vădastra ware shows striking originality, its decoration being remarkable for its wealth, perfection and inventiveness of design. Motifs consist mainly of spirals and meanders, arranged in metopes. The southern influence is revealed in 'face urns' similar to those from Troy I and II, and in the tradition of anthropomorphic plastic art.

Plate 14

Plate 15

Plate 12

Plate 13

THE BOIAN CULTURE

Plate 19

The Boian culture extended over much of both Romanian and Bulgarian territory (as far as the Balkans), its formation being determined by three factors, namely, the local substratum as represented by the southern Vădastra I, the Linear Pottery, and finally the Hamangia elements. Pottery with white-incrusted incised or excised decoration now begins a long period of evolution divisible into five phases. Black channelled ware and artistic ornamentation are found in all of these. Towards the end of the second phase there are clear signs of progress on the part of the Boian people. This can be seen, among other ways, in the transition from semi-subterranean to surface dwellings, and from dispersed to group settlements of a *tell* type. Copper objects become more common and the *tell*-settlements are fortified; for example, the Spanțov site (phase III) which is surrounded by a ditch 2 metres deep and 3–4 metres wide. Zoomorphic and anthropomorphic figurines derive from the Hamangian models. The basis of the economy is agriculture and stock-breeding. The largest Boian cemetery was found at Cernica. It contained Phase I burials, about 250 of which have been excavated. Grave furniture included pottery, stone axes, bone and flint tools, and personal ornaments (bracelets, beads, pendants) made of *Spondylus Pectunculus* and *Ostrea* shells. The bearers of this culture showed marked palaeo-Mediterranean affinities.

THE LATE NEOLITHIC: 2700–2200/1800 BC

Fig. 15

Thanks to developing material and spiritual resources during these centuries, tribes took a new step forward in well-being and social organization, thus managing to create the optimal living conditions for a primitive community. The *tell* becomes common. Settlements are usually fortified either by a ditch or by both a ditch and a rampart, which may point to hostilities between tribes at this time. The progressive spread of copper tools most certainly contributed to greater productivity. Slowly techniques for working copper and for exploiting the local copper ores are learnt. The late Neolithic tribes employed all main types of tools and weapons; and it is at this time that the boat-axe and the single-bladed axe as well as the shaft-hole axe become widely used. Gold objects coming from Transylvania also make their appearance.

REAPPEARANCE OF WIDER CULTURAL ZONES

Following the earlier splitting-up of cultures, wider cultural circles incorporating all the elements inherited from the past appear during this late phase. From the general historical point of view, the late Neolithic in the Carpatho-Danubian region and south-east Europe is distinguished by its magnificent painted ware, the designs of which are executed in various colours or in graphite. The economy is still based on localized agricultural communities and cultivation is everywhere increasing to a degree unknown in the past; however, towards the end of this phase pastoralism becomes progressively more important. A mixed economy is still prevalent since, at this time, the use of the plough had not yet been introduced. Increases in

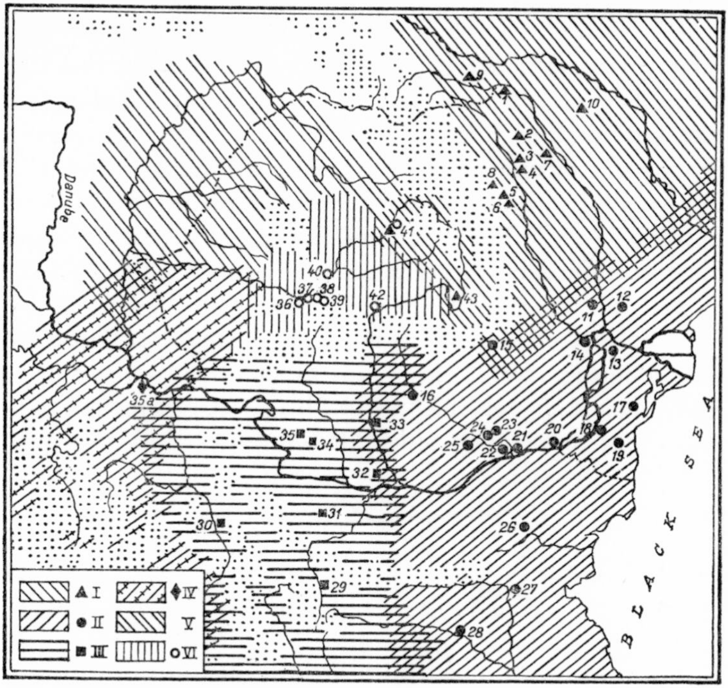

Fig. 15. The Late Neolithic in Romania

I Cucuteni culture; II Gumelniţa culture; III Sălcuţa culture; IV Vinča culture; V Tisa; VI Petreşti culture

1 Horodiştea
2 Truşeşti
3 Cucuteni
4 Hăbăşeşti
5 Izvoare
6 Traian
7 Larga Jijieia
8 Tîrpeşti
9 Lişcoteanca
10 Petreni
11 Stoicani
12 Vulcăneşti
13 Luncaviţa
14 Brăiliţa
15 Aldeni
16 Teiu
17 Baia
18 Cernavoda
19 Medgidia
20 Ciumeşti
21 Gumelniţa
22 Căscioarele
23 Glina
24 Vidra
25 Tangîru
26 Kodjadermen
27 Veselinovo
28 Marica
29 Gljniane
30 Bubanj
31 Krividol
32 Vădastra
33 Slatina (Strihăreţ)
34 Sălcuţa
35 Verbicioara
35a Vinča
36 Turdaş
37 Tărtăria
38 Pianul de Sus
39 Petreşti
40 Alba Iulia
41 Tg. Mureş
42 Caşolţ
43 Ariuşd

population are noticeable and sites are more numerous. Life becomes in general more stable and the depths of archaeological deposits indicates prolonged occupation of the settlements. Exchanges between tribes are intensified, though these were not established on a permanent basis until the Bronze Age. Although the different cultures are of heterogeneous origin they are linked by Aegeo-Mediterranean and Linear Pottery elements.

THE SĂLCUȚA CULTURE

The Sălcuța culture which arose in Oltenia, east Banat and neighbouring areas, corresponds to the Krivodol group in Bulgaria and that of Bubanj in Serbia. It derived directly from the Vinča culture with added Helladic and early Macedonian

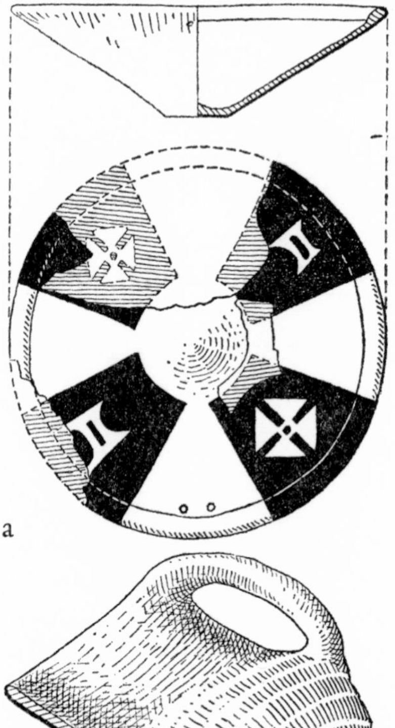

a

1 2

Fig. 16. a, Graphite painted dish, Sălcuța, Phase IIc of the Sălcuța culture; b, Askoi *from Verbicioara (Oltenia) Sălcuța culture. Width of a, 36cm. Height of b, 1 and 2, 5.7cm.*

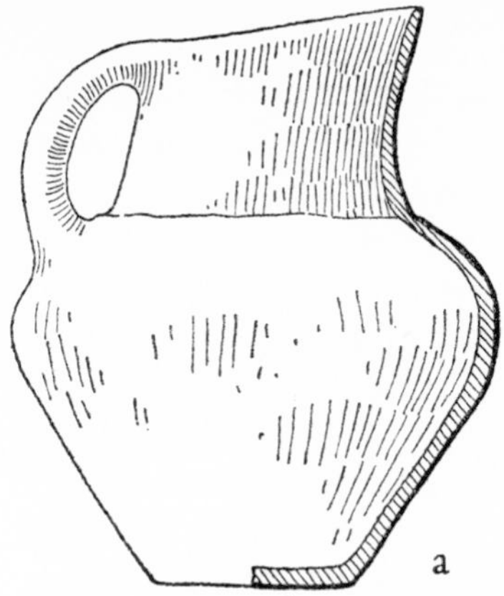

1

a

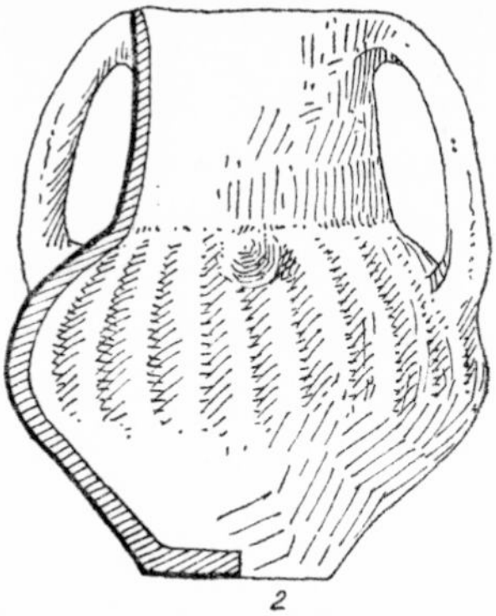

2

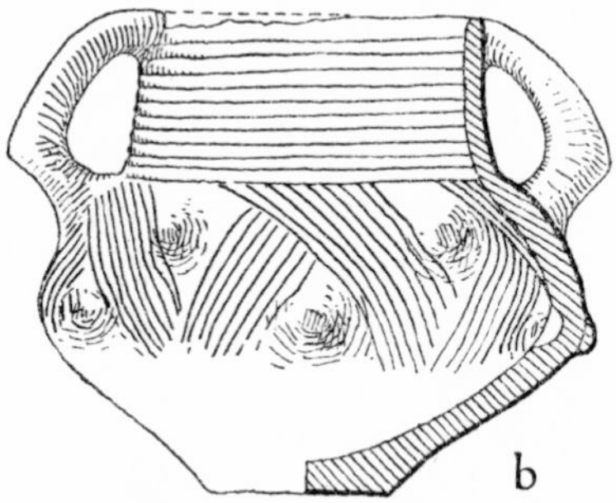

b

Fig. 17. a, Sălcuța pottery shapes from phase IIc (1) and phase III (2). b, Jar from Sălcuța, phase IV Sălcuța culture. Height of a, 1 20.5cm., 2 to scale. Height of b, 8.8cm.

Bronze Age elements. Further influences arrived from Troy. Sites are located on hills, as at 'Piscul Cornișorului' (Sălcuța), or on river terraces, whilst on the eastern periphery *tells* make their appearance. Occupation levels are still found in caves. Some sites have ditches and ramparts as defences. Flint, bone Plate 20
and horn tools become much more plentiful. More frequent finds of deer-antler hoes and querns attest an increase in plant-cultivation. Dwellings are aligned huts or large houses sometimes divided into two rooms. The shaft-hole axe comes into general use and in the third phase, the heavy copper wedge-shaped axe appears. Some pottery forms derive directly from the *Fig. 16*
Vinča culture, others show affinities with those from Gumelnița, while yet others can be related to prototypes from the south, such as the *askos* or the *Schnabelkanne* (beaked jug). Among the distinctive forms are two-handled cups, small *Fig. 17*

squat cups and bowls with thickened or incurving rims; decoration includes graphite painting and incrustation with colour. Within this culture four phases have been identified.

THE GUMELNIȚA CULTURE

Plates 22, 25, 26

Plate 23

Plate 21

Unlike the Sălcuța culture which was derived from the homogeneous Vinča material the Gumelnița culture was formed on heterogeneous foundations composed of elements from the southern Bulgarian Maritza culture, and from the Hamangia and Boian cultures. There are three main variants. Pontic, Balkano-Danubian and south Bulgarian. It passed through four phases. Settlements are in the form of *tells* surrounded on three sides by watercourses or located in areas given to swamping (Vărăști, Căscioarele, etc.), near lake-shores (Teiu); or on terrace promontories. The rectangular surface dwelling is the commonest form of habitation. Some houses have a porch of the *megaron* type. Clay models show ridged and gabled roofs. Some dwellings, as for example at Cucuteni, were constructed on platforms, which were built of tree-trunks, coated with clay and then burnt. Archaeological material includes arrowheads and

Fig. 18. Anthropomorphic bone figurines. a, from Sălcuța, Sălcuța culture phase IIb; b, from Sălcuța, Sălcuța culture phase I(1), from Pietrele, Gumelnița culture phase II(2). Height of a, 5.5cm.; of b, 1.8cm. (1) and 16cm. (2)

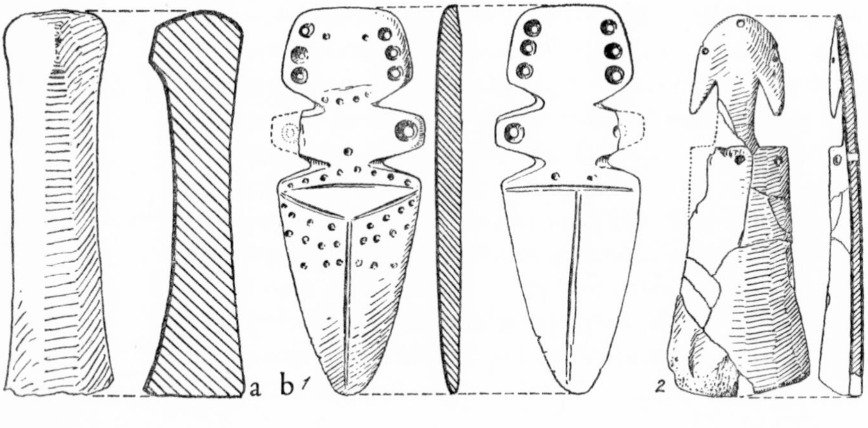

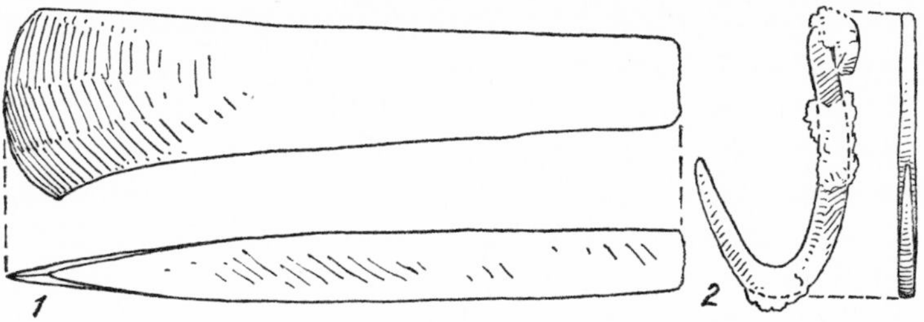

Fig. 19. *1, Copper chisel from Sălcuţa, Sălcuţa culture phase III; 2, copper fish-hook from Pietrele, Gumelniţa culture phase II. Length of 1, 13.9cm.; height of 2, 5cm.*

spearheads, heavy flint axes, deer-antler hoes, bone and horn chisels, needles, etc. The number of bronze axes and knife blades multiplies. Pure copper is employed for making these objects. The Vidra-type axe is widely used; and it is from this type that the battle-axe is derived. The diffusion of gold ornaments at this period over an area covered by various different cultures confirms the existence of very far-reaching trade. Knowledge of spinning and weaving is amply attested. New technical improvements are introduced into the making of pottery: special ovens are now used for firing pots. Graphite painting and crusted ware are found as well as types similar to Sălcuţa ware. Clay and bone anthropomorphic figurines, whose origin can be found in Hamangian models, are very frequent in deposits. The dead are interred in a contracted position; from the anthropological point of view the Mediterranean type is prevalent.

Fig. 19

Fig. 18

THE CUCUTENI CULTURE

In the north and north-east of the country the Cucuteni or Ariuşd-Cucuteni-Tripolje culture develops, characterized by its magnificent painted ware. Four main phases have been distinguished, preceded by a pre-Cucuteni level. These are referred to as either Cucuteni I, II, III, and IV; or alternatively as Cucuteni A, A-B, B, and the final Cucuteni culture. It is now

Fig. 20. Detail of the human figure painted on a pot from Traian (Plate 30), Cucuteni culture phase II (AB)

possible to identify the origin and evolution of this culture and its affinities with other civilizations. The pre-Cucuteni culture developed from a number of heterogeneous elements including those of the Linear Pottery Boian and Hamangia cultures, Criș survivals and influences from the Lower Bug. Flint tools at this period remain microlithic and figurines are distinctive: quite a primitive version of a 'thinker'-type figurine was recovered from the site at Tîrpești (Moldavia). Cucuteni sites are fortified with one or two ditches and in extent sometimes cover as much as 15 acres (6 hectares), and they are fairly densely populated. Houses are arranged either in parallel rows (Trușești) or in circles (Hăbășești). These rectangular dwellings are erected on platforms which are built either of tree-trunks coated with clay and then burnt, or of undressed stones. The archaeological legacy left by these tribes is large and varied. It includes curved flint knives, stone shaft-hole battle-axes, deer-antler hoes, and various bone and copper objects (wedge-axes, knife blades, battle-axes, awls, daggers, personal ornaments), as well as gold jewellery. The outstanding achievement of the Cucuteni folk is their painted ware. Bichrome and trichrome decoration, painted before firing, is a technique adopted by the Ariușd tribes from the Petrești people. Motifs painted on Cucuteni include both positive or negative spirals on a red or white background, meanders, etc. During phase II (A-B), painted motifs are arranged to form patterns. At this period pottery made of a fabric mixed with sand and ground shells and ornamented with cord impressions first appears. During phase III (B) black designs are painted on a yellowish-brown or whitish background. Painted designs later become rare and line motifs, such as the 'net' prevail. During the fourth and last phase (Horodiștea-Foltești) painted ware is scarce, and finally disappears with the rise of corded ware. The following distinctive forms are found in Cucuteni pottery: conical goblets, amphorae, fruit stands, 'Swedish helmet' lids, polychrome ladles, etc. Most of the

Plates 28, 29

Plate 30

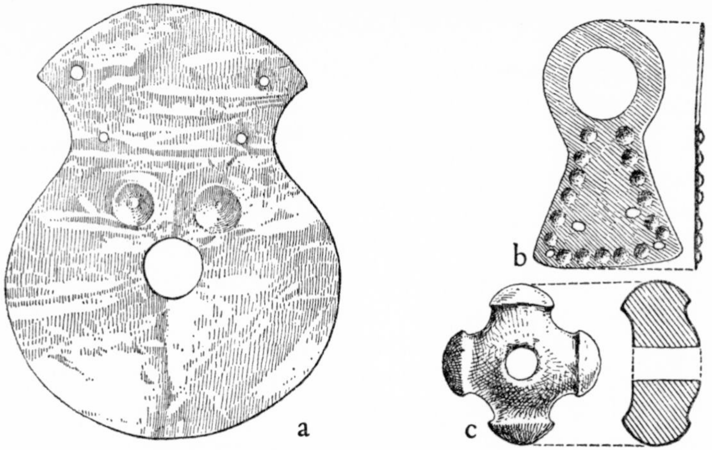

Fig. 21. a, Large gold pendant from the Moigrad hoard; b, gold pendant from Traian, Cucuteni culture phase II (AB); c, knobbed stone mace-head from a tomb at Decia (Mureşului). Height of a, 22.6cm.; of b, 2.65cm.; diameter of c, 7cm.

figurines represent females. The most frequent is the 'violin' type in clay and even copper, apparently related to the Cycladic and Trojan models. The religious beliefs of these tribes are also attested by the 'altar' from Truşeşti in the form of two very stylized human figures. It would appear that the dead of the Cucuteni culture were inhumed. At Traian, tombs were discovered containing ritual burials belonging to Cucuteni II. Although the general anthropological structure of these populations is heterogeneous, studies have revealed the predominance of a Mediterranean type. *Fig. 20* *Fig. 21* Plate 27

With regard to the absolute chronology of the Cucuteni culture, the following radiocarbon dates are available: Cucuteni III (B) from Valea Lupului – 3000 ± 60 (GrN 1982); Cucuteni IIc (A3) from Hăbăşeşti – 3380 ± 80 (GrN 1985). These dates, like that of Gumelniţa – 3410 ± 70 (Grn 1987), raise a number of problems concerning the chronology of these cultures and their relationship with the Aegean world and Asia Minor.

THE PETREŞTI CULTURE

In central Transylvania there developed during the late Neolithic a culture using painted ware, known as 'painted ware of the Transylvanian Group'. The technique of the Starčevo-type painted ware passed directly from the Turdaş culture to the Petreşti culture, which in turn handed it down to the bearers of the Cucuteni-Tripolje culture. This solves the much discussed problem as to the origin of the Cucuteni-Tripolje painted ware. Settlements are located on the lower terraces of watercourses; remains of occupation have also been found in caves. Habitations may be in the form of huts or semi-subterranean dwellings; sometimes houses are raised on piles. Tools are mainly of flint; copper is less common. Undecorated ware of the Turdaş type survives for a considerable time. Four main phases can be distinguished in the development. In the proto-Petreşti phase trichrome painted ware has already appeared. Motifs or decorative elements are outlined in black (*Rahmenstil*). Simple bands, spirals and meanders form the basis of decoration as well as combined spiral and meander designs. At a later stage graphite painting was also employed. From Tîrgu-Mureş there comes a magnificent gold pendant, for which analogies can be found in the Gumelniţa and Cucuteni zones. The dead were buried in a contracted position, the Mediterranean anthropological type being predominant. At the site in the locality of 'Poiana în Pisc' at Caşolţ, near Sibiu, two ritual pits were discovered containing the remains of sacrifices and ceremonial offerings.

Plate 24

TRANSITION TO THE BRONZE AGE

The Carpatho-Danubian zone was destined to play an essential part during this period of transition, and in the great linguistic phenomenon leading to the Indo-European movement just beginning in these regions at that time. The bearers of the Cernavoda civilization, arriving from the south and from Anatolia, were Indo-European, as were those who brought the 'Ochre-grave' culture; these two cultures came into contact in the Caucasus and along the west and north coasts of the Black

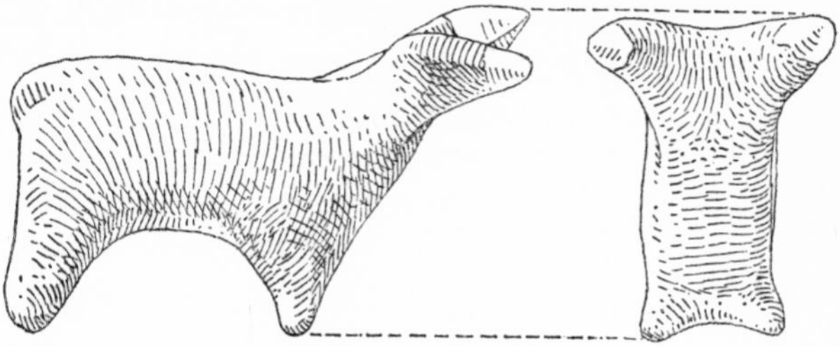

Fig. 22. Zoomorphic figurine from Govora-Sat, Coţofeni culture. Height, 3.1cm.

Sea. From north of the Black Sea and the wooded steppes, groups of nomadic herdsmen, folk of the Ochre-grave culture, penetrated into Romanian territory by successive stages. They were assimilated by the indigenous population, while at the same time enriching local cultures and accelerating the process of Neolithic disintegration. It is they who introduced the use of the domestic horse and bronze and silver objects into the area of their penetration. They reinforced the pastoral economy and the spread of Indo-European languages. At this time the wide area covered by the Coţofeni culture occupied an important place. During the last part of its development, with the late *Furchenstichkeramik* style and that of the final Vučedol phase,

Fig. 22

Fig. 23

Fig. 23. Decorated Vučedol ware from Moldova Veche. Heights, 10cm. (1) and 10.2cm. (2)

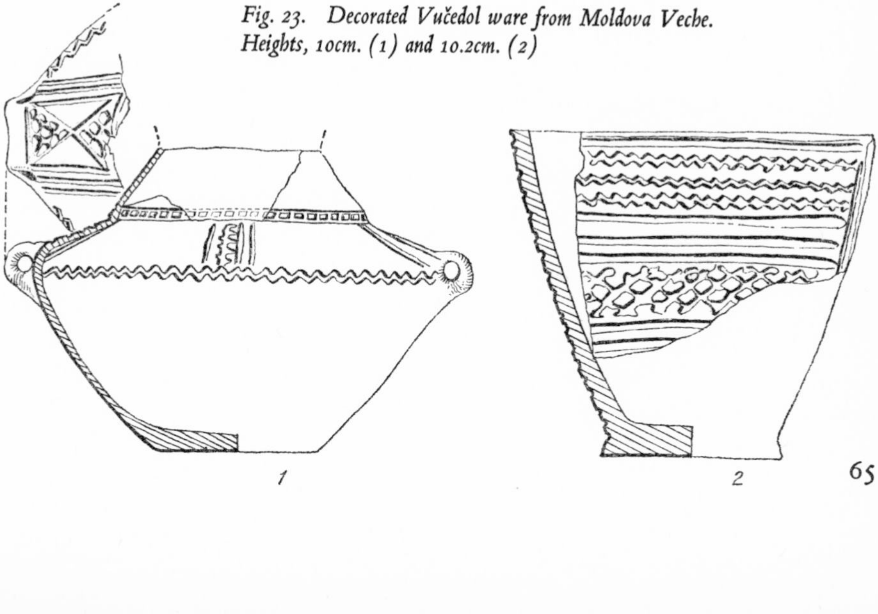

this culture reaches the threshold of the Bronze Age. The Coțofeni material overlies the Sălcuța IV level, and, in south-east Transylvania, the latest Ariușd-Cucuteni level. The economy takes on a more marked pastoral character, although agriculture still continued. Sites were located on plateaux in the mountainous region, but some are found in the Danube valley or in its immediate neighbourhood. Occasionally they are perched on high rocky summits, or surrounded by ditches and earth ramparts. Battle-axes are still in use. The most characteristic pottery shapes are the strap-handled cups with an oblique rim. The Helladic element, and the southern influence in general, appears not only in the decorative motifs but also in the forms – the *askos* is a case in point. Decoration consisting of lentil-grain impressed patterns (*Linsenkeramik*) appears only at a later stage. The predominant funerary rite was inhumation, although cremation was also practised.

In the course of this period several groups from the Danube belonging to the Vučedol culture penetrated into Romanian territory. An extremely rich site has been identified on the Moldova Veche Isle in Banat.

Semi-nomadic groups of herdsmen arrived from the regions of Volhynia and Podolia: these were the bearers of the 'Globular-amphorae' or 'Cist-grave' culture. Some passed from Moldavia to Transylvania and advanced by infiltration towards the Danube, penetrating as far as Serbia. In addition to the pottery ornamented with cord-impressions, there are bangles and gold buckles of beautiful filigree-work, like those from the double tomb at Dolhești (Moldavia). This particular type of cist grave was inherited by the Glina and Monteoru folk of the Bronze Age.

Chapter V

The Bronze Age

THE ROMANIAN BRONZE AGE IN ITS SETTING OF SOUTH-EAST AND CENTRAL EUROPE

THE BRONZE AGE CULTURES of Romania in general form an integral part of the south-east and central European setting, and this unity is attested in both the material and the spiritual sphere. Ethnically, the bearers of these cultures can, from the Middle Bronze Age onwards, be regarded as proto-Thracians, the ancestors of the Thracians. However, the area covered by the Thracian bronze culture exceeded the frontiers of Romania.

Archaeological discoveries in Romania suggest that, during the Bronze Age, Thracian tribes of the Carpathians and the Danube established relations and extensive trade exchanges with communities in central and eastern Europe, as well as with peoples in the Aegean and Mediterranean areas, particularly the Helladic and Mycenaean world. Bronze Age conditions had prevailed in these latter areas for several centuries, and had actively influenced the formation of Carpatho-Danubian cultural styles. Thus the cultural life of the Romanian Bronze Age communities, although showing certain distinctive features, forms part of the historical process then taking place in a territory which was appreciably greater in extent than Europe. The Carpatho-Danubian Bronze Age cultures themselves reflect the merging of several influences, and at the same time they supply a link between central and eastern Europe and the east Mediterranean Basin. Similar convergent influences also gave rise to the particularities of local styles, thus giving the Carpatho-Danubian Bronze cultures their distinctive aspect. This is strikingly illustrated by bronze metallurgy. Recent discoveries have, in fact, revealed the existence, in all the Carpatho-Danubian zone, of numerous workshops which continued in use during the Hallstatt I and II periods. It is quite possible, therfore, to speak of a Carpatho-Danubian bronze metallurgy.

CHRONOLOGY AND CLASSIFICATION

Fig. 24 One of the first tasks of Romanian archaeology has been the stratigraphical classification of cultures. Only when this has been achieved can a systematic chronology be worked out, since that employed in east central Europe is not really applicable to the Carpatho-Danubian region. In this area there is no break in the development of the Bronze Age after phases C and D; on the contrary, there is continuous progress right down to the local Iron Age.

Taking into account the origin and evolution of each culture, and the general historical processes which affect the local Bronze Age, four main periods can be distinguished and their chronology established. The oldest culture, linked to the Aegeo-Mediterranean South, can be dated to about 2200 BC, at a time when the Cernavoda culture appeared in the Lower Danube. The maturing and the full development of the Middle and Late Bronze Ages can be dated to about 1600 to 1300 BC. The period from 1300 to 1200 BC covers the final development and the transition phase, and 1200 BC marks the end of the Bronze Age. Although this began earlier in some regions than in others, it finished simultaneously in all areas. It follows, therefore, that the transition to primitive plough-agriculture using a wooden or horn ploughshare took place at different dates in different regions. It is, however, important to realize that, except for the Cernavoda culture, the Carpatho-Danubian material is local in origin.

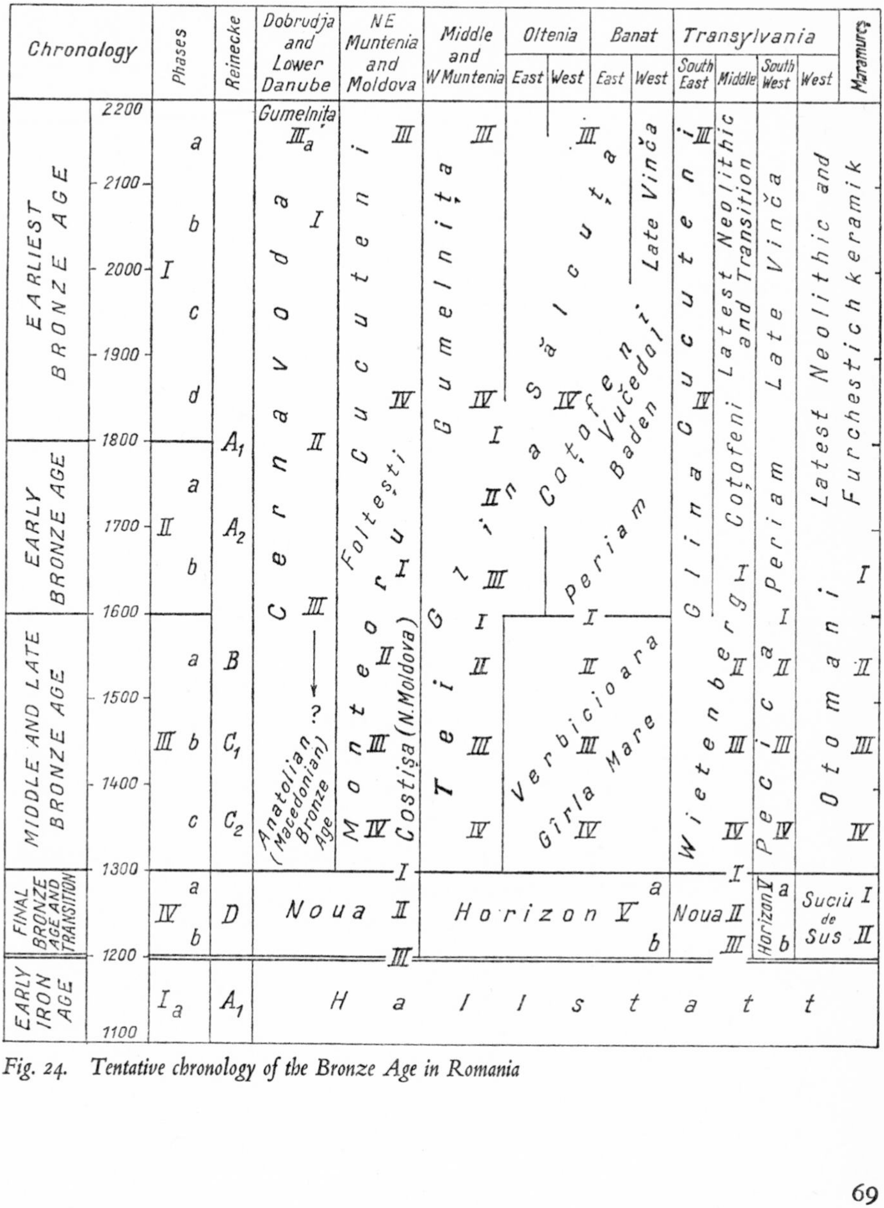

Fig. 24. Tentative chronology of the Bronze Age in Romania

THE EARLY BRONZE AGE (BI, II) 2200–1600 BC

THE CERNAVODA CULTURE

The Cernavoda culture, identified in 1956, extends over the whole Dobrudja region and in a wide belt north of the Danube. Parallels for it can be found in the Ezero culture in Bulgaria and the Donja Slatina culture in Yugoslavia. High ground was chosen for the sites, which are occasionally fortified with ditches and earth stockades. Other settlements with dispersed dwellings and without fortifications are located on the lower terraces of rivers. Others again are situated on the earlier Romanian and Bulgarian Gumelnița *tells*, or in the immediate neighbourhood of Neolithic sites. The pottery, metal tools, and the way of life of these folk, and even their anthropological type, all point to the Aegeo-Anatolian character of this culture, which retains certain Neolithic elements such as the clay figurine from Cernavoda. Flint, stone and bone tools are widely used. Metal tools and weapons of copper and bronze distributed

Fig. 25

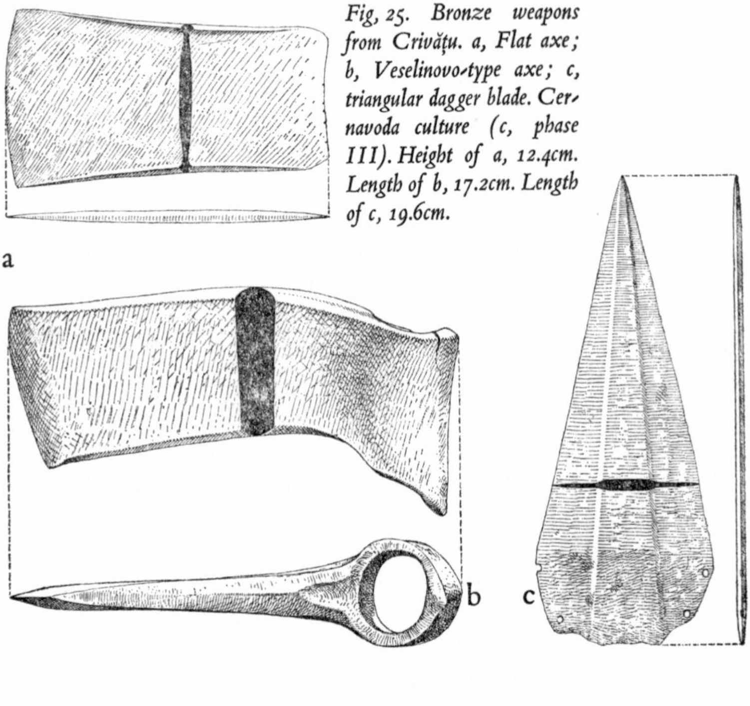

Fig, 25. Bronze weapons from Crivățu. a, Flat axe; b, Veselinovo-type axe; c, triangular dagger blade. Cernavoda culture (c, phase III). Height of a, 12.4cm. Length of b, 17.2cm. Length of c, 19.6cm.

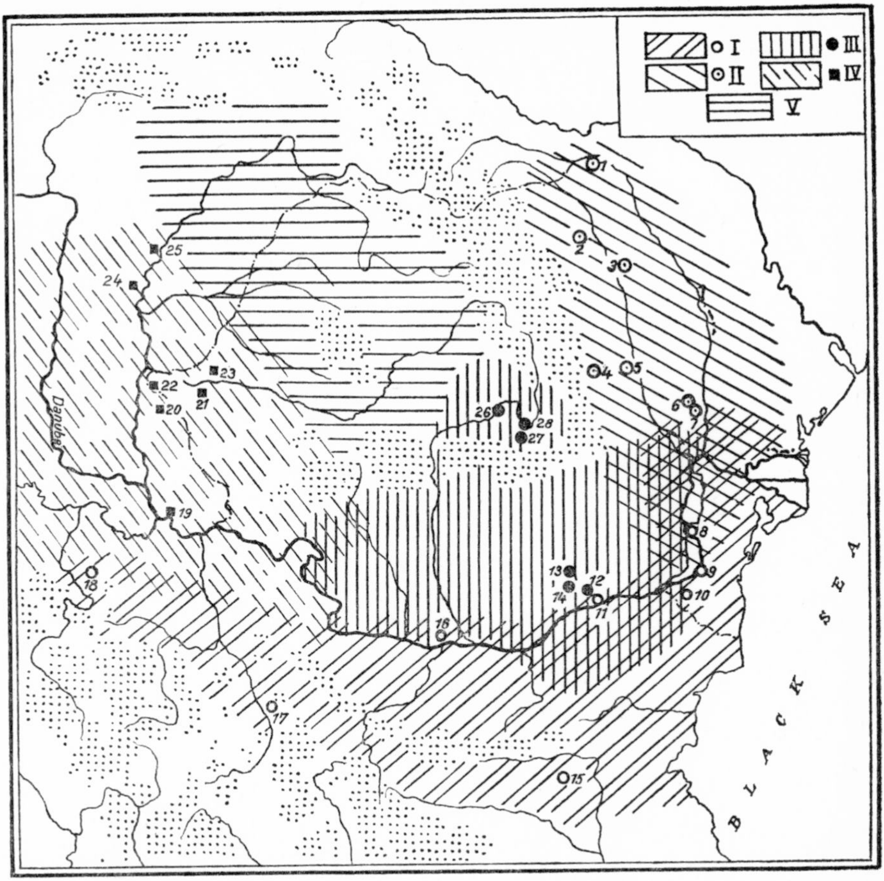

Fig. 26. Early Bronze Age in Romania

I Cernavoda culture; II Foltești culture; III Glina culture; IV Periam-Mokrin culture; V Final Neolithic

1 Horodiștea
2 Dolheștii Mari
3 Hăbășești
4 Bogdănești
5 Mîndrișca
6 Foltești
7 Stoicani
8 Hîrșova
9 Cernavoda
10 Adamclissi
11 Oltenița
12 Glina
13 Crivățu
14 Vidra
15 Ezerovo
16 Celei
17 Donja Slatina
18 Belotić
19 Pančevo
20 Mokrin
21 Periam
22 Beba Veche
23 Pecica
24 Nagyrev
25 Tószeg
26 Cuciulata
27 Schneckenberg
28 Ariușd

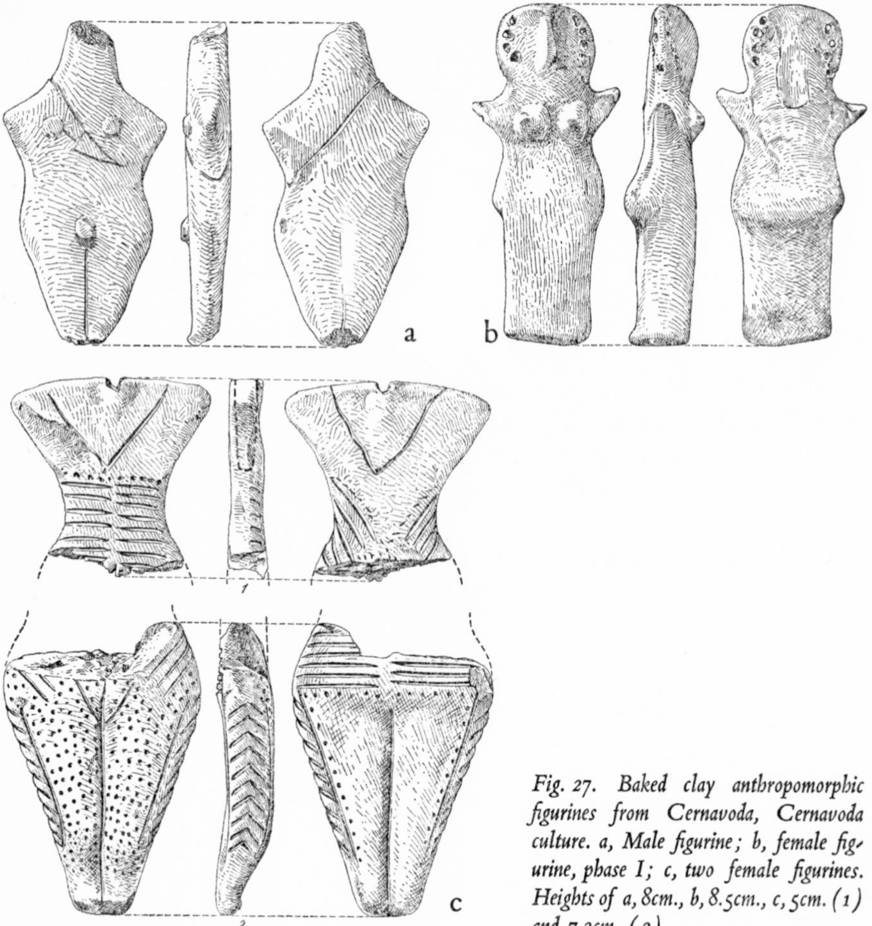

Fig. 27. Baked clay anthropomorphic figurines from Cernavoda, Cernavoda culture. a, Male figurine; b, female figurine, phase I; c, two female figurines. Heights of a, 8cm., b, 8.5cm., c, 5cm. (1) and 7.2cm. (2)

throughout the area of this culture are particularly important, because of the early penetration into the Lower Danube in this late period of southern types such as the single-blade shaft-hole *Fig. 25* axe of a Veselinovo type, which recalls the Baniabic type. The flat axe with slightly raised edges was also a characteristic

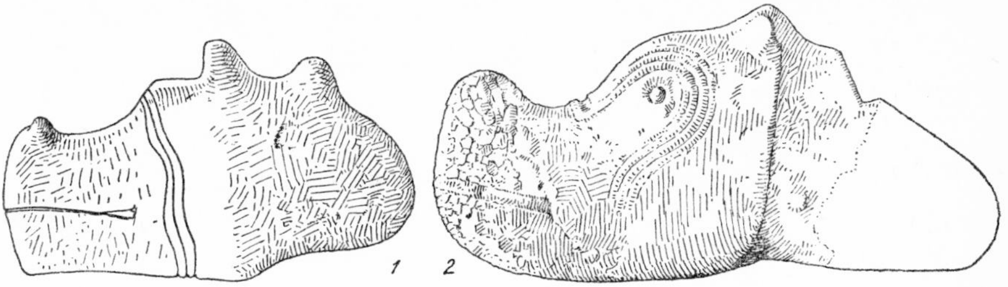

Fig. 28. Sceptre-heads, 1 from Sălcuța, and 2 from Casimcea. Cernavoda culture. Lengths: 13 cm. (1) and 17cm. (2)

weapon; examples have been found at Crivăț and elsewhere. Several different types of dagger blades have also been recovered: (a) those with a narrow hilt which show analogies with a type found in the north Pontic steppes or those of the Nitra or Otomani (early phase) group in Slovakia; (b) the triangular three-riveted blade (for example from Ghizdaru, in Muntenia); (c) the blade with four rivets, comparable to a series of Early Helladic (E.H.), Cycladic or Anatolian daggers. A similar

Fig. 29. Distribution of the six zoomorphic 'sceptres'

type has been recovered from a cist grave in the mountainous region of Muntenia. This Aegean influence can also be recognized in a clay figurine of a man on whose chest is incised a drawing of a solid-hilted dagger of a type found in the Mycenaean 'Royal Tomb' horizon. Among the pottery the fine grey pseudo-Minyan or proto-Minyan ware is of particular interest. Decoration includes notched cordons, incised designs, occasional lentil-grain patterns, parallel channels or twisted-
Fig. 27 cord impressions. The series of female figurines with detached heads can be classified with the Thessalian type. Another group comprises female figurines with a rather exaggerated
Figs. 28, 29 torso. The group of six sceptre-heads belong to this same culture; and a similar sceptre-head was recovered from the tomb at Casimcea. The economy was mixed, with stock-breeding the main activity. Numerous spindle-whorls show that spinning and weaving were practised. The dead were interred in a contracted position and sprinkled with red ochre. Analysis of human remains has confirmed that the bearers of the culture in question differed from the north Pontic 'Ochre-grave' folk; they belonged to an anthropological type frequently encountered in the east Mediterranean.

Three phases of evolution have been distinguished, and a fourth may be assumed. The first phase, in which the domestic horse first appears and cord-impressed patterns decorate the pots, has been dated by C14 to 2495 ±100 and 2310 ±100 BC. The north Pontic 'Ochre-grave' horizon, discovered south of the Danube, is more recent; C14 analysis of wood from the Caemurlia de Jos grave gave a date of 2140 ±160 BC, thus confirming that the Mediterranean element arrived before the eastern-pastoral factor. In trying to identify this culture we are faced with a number of problems, over and above those concerning the beginnings and origin of the Bronze Age in the Lower Danube, or the distribution of the domestic horse and cord-ornamented pottery. In actual fact its extension towards

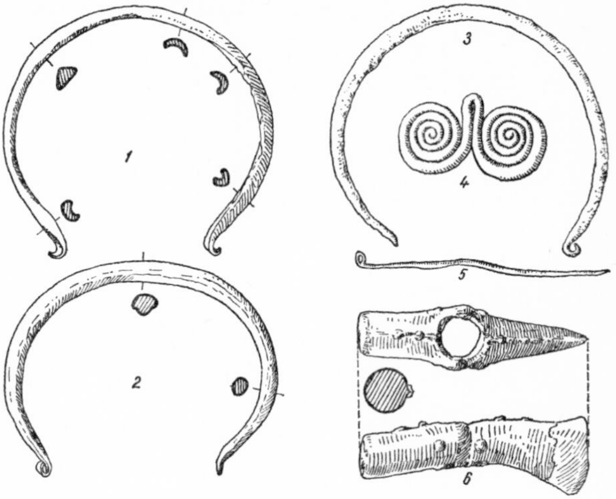

Fig. 30. Early Bronze Age material. 1,2, Copper bar torques from Deva, about 13cm. wide. 3–5, Torque, double spiral ornament and pin from Periam and 6, copper axe with a cylindrical butt, from the Tufa hoards. Width of 1,2: about 13cm. Length of 6, 11,3cm.

the Iron Gates and into Serbia has raised the problem of its contacts with the Baden-Pecel culture and the part played by the Cernavoda culture where east Mediterranean influences on central Europe at that time are concerned. Naturally, attention must also be focused on the Indo-European problem in the Lower Danube, as well as on that of the spread of grey proto-Minyan ware towards Greece.

THE GLINA CULTURE

This important culture, long known as Glina III – Schneckenberg, is the result of a synthesis of heterogeneous elements derived mainly from the last Gumelniţa phase, with added external elements. The most active element in this culture was the Cernavoda which transmitted the cultural traits of Mediterranean origin, such as channelled ware, 'Hollow-wart' decoration, the Veselinovo axe and various type of daggers, as well as the knowledge of some bronze-working techniques. Influences from the east and the 'Globular-amphorae' culture also played their part in this process. Sites are found either in the same places as those of the Gumelniţa or Ariuşd-Cucuteni

Fig. 31

Fig. 30

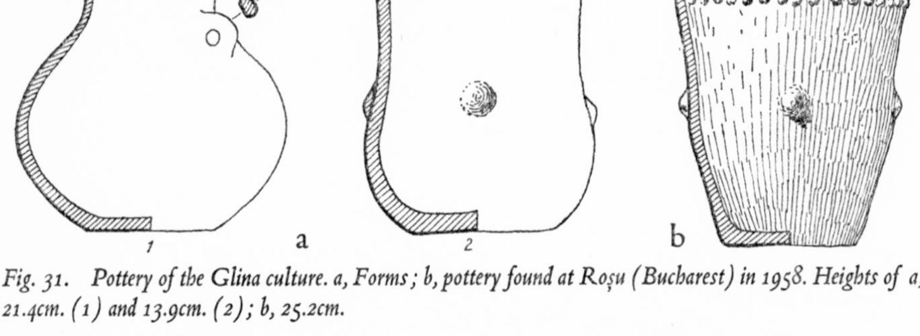

Fig. 31. Pottery of the Glina culture. a, Forms; b, pottery found at Roșu (Bucharest) in 1958. Heights of a, 21.4cm. (1) and 13.9cm. (2); b, 25.2cm.

people, or on the more easily defensible hill-tops where huts were erected. Tools are mostly made of stone, and include small flat axes, shaft-hole axes, battle-axes, curved flint or sandstone knives. In addition there are grooved hammers for breaking ores or rock salt, and flint arrowheads. Copper and bronze objects are relatively few, but from this early period, they are also to be found north of the Carpathians; one example is the conical-headed pin from the Dealul Șprenghelui site (Brașov). In the area covered by this culture Baniabic axes, and some gold-leaf personal ornaments are found. There is a variety of pottery, including bowls of varying depth, and askoi, with single-handed pitchers and cups with two handles predominating. The four-wheeled cart of southern origin is now found north of the Carpathians, as the discovery at Cuciulata (Transylvania) of a tiny clay model bears out. Zoomorphic and anthropomorphic figurines are also found. Ceramic decoration includes incised lines, cordons, hollow warts (nipples), etc. The dead were buried in cists in a contracted position. The economy remains of a mixed type although pastoralism still plays a preponderant part. Three phases have been identified in the evolution of this culture, which itself helped in forming the Tei, Monteoru, Verbicioara and Wietenberg cultures.

Fig. 32. Flint arrowheads from Brașov. Glina culture. Length of 1, 6cm., 2 to scale

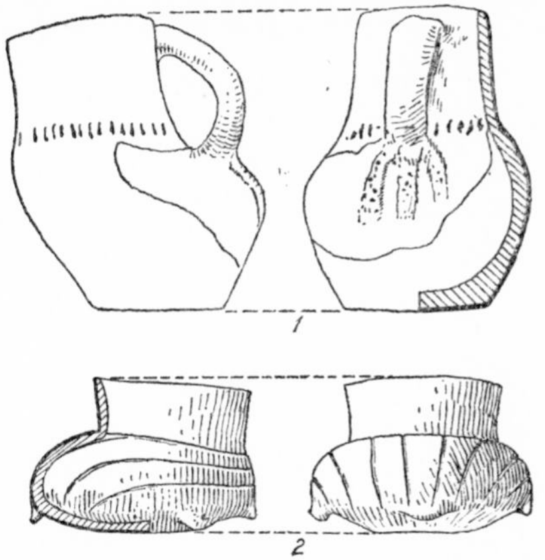

Fig. 33. Askoi. *From Foltești (Foltești horizon) (1) and Stoicani (Gumelnița culture) (2). Height of 1, 11.2cm.; of 2, 8cm.*

THE FOLTEȘTI CULTURE

In Moldavia at this time the Foltești style develops. It derives from the immediately preceding culture which was the final phase of the Cucuteni. The type site was surrounded by a defence ditch. The material includes elements which are similar to and contemporary with those of Glina and Cernavoda (II), such as the Foltești askos-vase, datable to the Early Bronze Age. *Fig. 33* The vase from Cunești also provides a point of reference. The most frequent pottery shapes are ovoid pitchers with cylindrical necks, and cups with everted rims. Tools to be noted are awls and chinels, curved stone knives, and baked clay spindle-whorls; zoomorphic figurines are ornamented with lines of incised dots. At Bogdănești the Foltești layer underlies the Monteoru Ib (Ic3) material but it overlies the 'Cist-grave' horizon. *Fig. 34* It is a culture characteristic of the Bronze Age in south, central and north Moldavia.

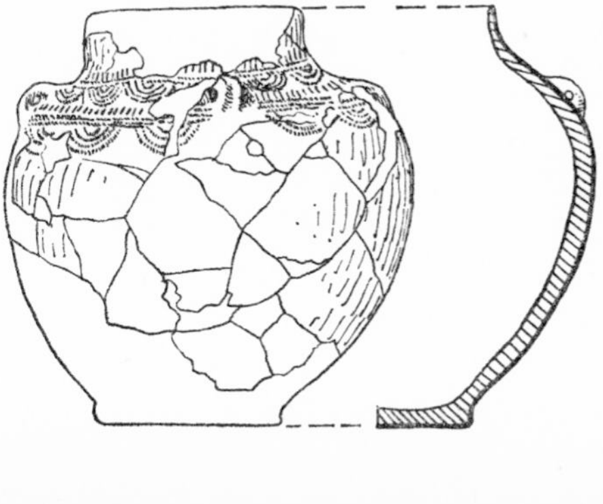

Fig. 34. Jar from Delbeștii Mari (Moldavia), 'cist-grave' culture. Height, 22.5cm.

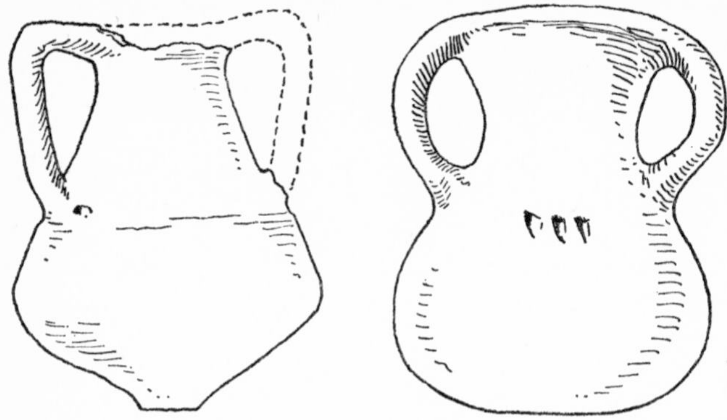

Fig. 35. Pottery forms from Periam, Periam culture. Height, about 9cm. (Arad Museum)

THE PERIAM HORIZON

Fig. 35

Closely associated with the material from the cultural strata and substrata of the Iron Gates and the neighbouring areas of Yugoslavia and south-east Hungary is the new horizon which appeared in south-west Romania. The most distinctive pottery shapes are single- or double-handled cups, and a variant of the clepsydra with a cylindrical neck and globular body. Decoration, generally of a tectonic type, consists of incised parallel lines, arranged in metopes and triglyphs. Outstanding metal objects are double spiral ornaments of copper and bronze, torques, pins (*Rollennadel*), bangles, etc. These people lived in huts; at Periam, excavations have revealed a house apparently built on a *megaron* plan. Three cultures had their starting point in this horizon: Vattina-Gîrla Mare, Pecica and Verbicioara.

THE REGIONS OF WEST ROMANIA

At present the Early Bronze Age is not well defined in west Romania. Probably here, and to some extent in central Transylvania, the final Neolithic and transitional styles persisted and developed during the Early Bronze Age, as they did in the Vučedol and the *Furchenstichkeramik* cultures.

THE MIDDLE AND LATE BRONZE AGE (BIII) 1600–1300 BC

Fig. 36

The transition from the Early to the Middle and Late Bronze Ages took place around 1600 BC, when conditions favoured new cultural alignments. The economy was almost equally

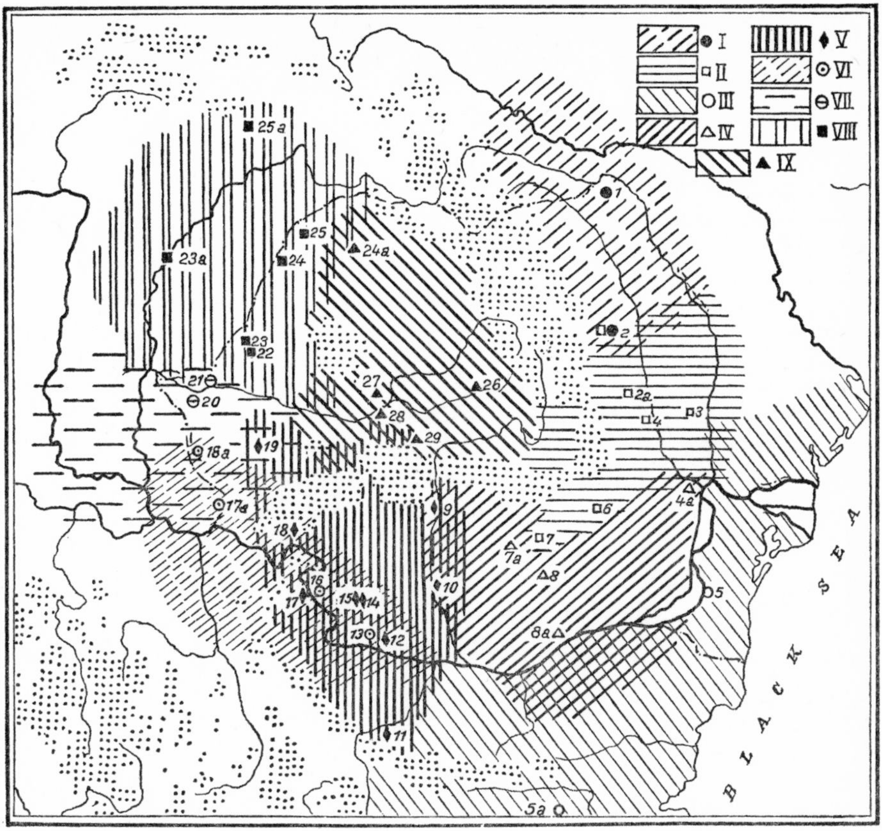

Fig. 36. The Middle and Late Bronze Age in Romania

I Costișa culture; II Monteoru culture; III Cernavoda culture; IV Tei culture; V Verbicioara culture; VI Gîrla Mare culture; VII Pecica culture; VIII Otomani culture; IX Wietenberg culture

1 Corlăteni
2 Costișa
2a Mîndrișca
3 Balintești
4 Poiana
4a Baldovinești
5 Cernavoda
5a Ezerovo
6 Monteoru
7 Tinosu
7a Perșinari
8 Tei
8a Oinac (Giurgiu)
9 Vlădești
10 Slatina
11 Devetaki
12 Săpata
13 Cîrna
14 Orodel
15 Verbicioara
16 Gîrla Mare
17 Kladovo
17a Vattina
18 Băile Herculane
18a Cruceni
19 Vișagu
20 Periam
21 Pecica
22 Vărșand
23 Socodor
23a Tószeg
24 Sîntion
24a Dersila
25 Otomani
25a Barca
26 Wietenberg
27 Țelna
28 Pianul de Jos
29 Ocna Sibiului

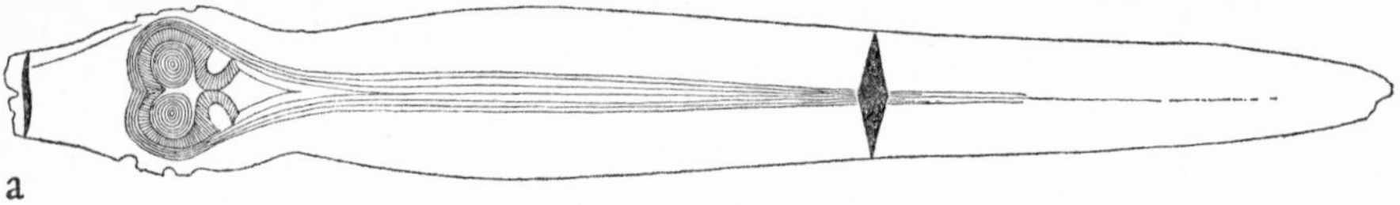

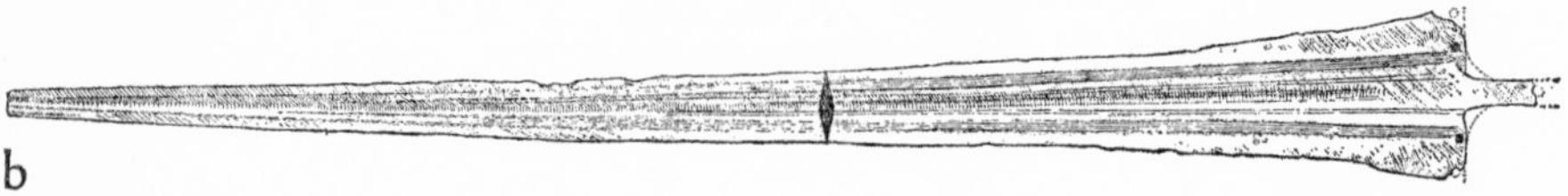

Fig. 37. a, Boian-type sword from Şincai, middle Bronze Age; b, Mycenaean rapier sword from Roşiorii-de-Vede. Length of a, 30.8cm.; of b, 67.8cm.

agricultural and pastoral, although certain groups were already showing a tendency towards one or the other of these activities. At this time the old traditions and ways of life of the Thracians were being re-shaped by new influences. A significant example of this is the revival of the spiral motif, which, although it was perhaps stimulated by the influences of the Mycenaean civilization, is also to be found in earlier local artifacts. Technical knowledge concerning bronze-working slowly spread over all the Carpatho-Danubian region, and the value of the rich copper ores of Transylvania, Oltenia and Dobrudja began to be appreciated. The axe (as a Thracian tool and weapon), the sword and the sickle – found in various forms in all the local cultures and dispersed by trade exchanges to the mouth of the Oder and the Bug – all developed remarkably in the Thracian metallurgical centres. These same workshops also produced various personal ornaments and bronze vessels; and they continued to work after the end of Bronze III, during period IV and even Hallstatt I and II, in order to supply the increasing demand created by wars and barter. The means of transport had been improved, the four-wheeled waggon having come into general use (see the small baked-clay model belonging to the Wietenberg culture shown on page 95); the archaeological evidence shows that horses and oxen were used for drawing both carts and ploughs. Metal was not yet used for ploughshares, which were still made of animal horn or possibly of

Fig. 37

Fig. 46

wood. Agriculture reached a new stage in its development. On both sides of the Carpathians and the Danube, metal ores circulated not only in the form of ingot-torques as in the Early Bronze Age, but also as rough cakes of a specific size. Mention must also be made at this point of the hoards of ingot-bars at Deva and Maglavit in Oltenia. As a result trade and barter, some tribes came into possession of faience and amber beads, as well as various types of Mycenaean weapons such as the so-called rapiers from Roșiorii de Vede, from Transylvania and elsewhere. Not only were the local copper ore deposits exploited but also the salt and gold of Transylvania and the amber of Buzău, known as 'Black Sea amber'. Spinning and weaving were practised by all tribes, but varied in importance from one culture to another. One of the main features of society at this time was metal-working characterized by specialization at its different stages, from the extraction of the ores to the finishing process of a given type of tool, weapon or ornament.

Fig. 30

Fig. 37b

Fig. 38. a, Three solid gold axes from the Țufalău hoard, 1, 15cm. long, others to scale; b, bronze axe with an enlarged and finely decorated butt from Ernei in the Apa-Țufalău horizon, Bronze III

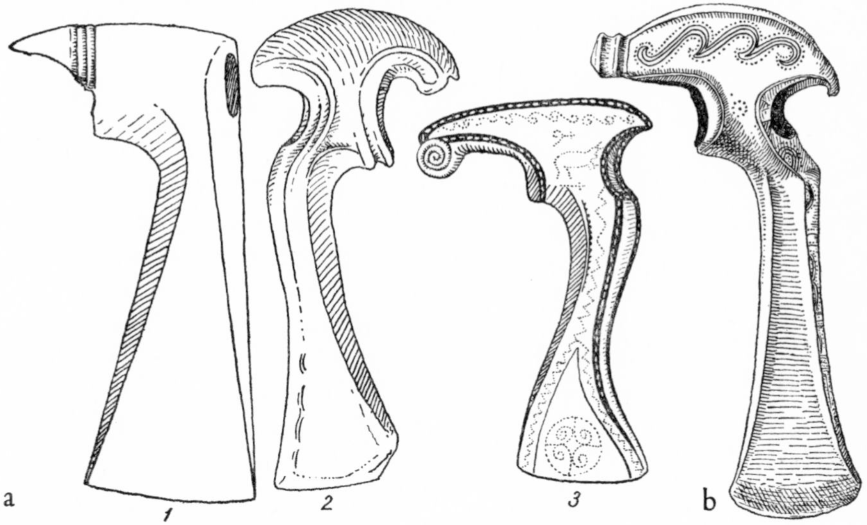

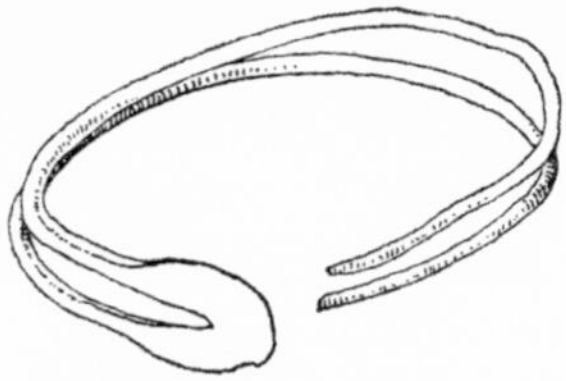

Fig. 39. Gold bangle from the Ţigănaşi hoard, Gîrla Mare culture. Maximum diameter, 14cm.

Fig. 38
Plate 39
Fig. 39

Societies themselves at this time were undergoing structural changes. Gold hoards, such as those from Ţufalău or Ţigănaşi (Oltenia), as well as others containing a great variety of objects and a large quantity of gold, most certainly represented the collective wealth of the tribe or groups of tribes which were already beginning to form. Furthermore, the wealth of grave furniture from certain tombs indicates the gradual movement towards social class-divisions, which had however not yet essentially weakened the foundations of community ownership. The increase in labour productivity and the growth in wealth following pillaging wars was also leading in this direction.

THE TEI CULTURE

In Dobrudja and along the banks of the Danube, the Cernavoda culture continued to develop during Bronze III, showing certain southern aspects which were also discovered north of the Danube as, for example, at Cuneşti near Călăraşi. Nevertheless, in the Muntenian plain, a new culture, the Tei (named after the Lake of Tei, Bucharest), comes to light; it is concentrated in the centre of Muntenia, but reaches almost to the hilly region. It was derived from Glina and Cernavoda stock. Its earliest phase was identified in the Căţelu district of the town of Bucharest in 1960; its Cernavoda element is clearly seen in the fabric, shapes and decoration of the pottery. The last survivals of the 'Ochre-grave' folk from the Muntenian plain were also absorbed into the Tei culture. Finally, the links with the Aegeo-Mediterranean world, in this case the Mycenaean civilization and the Macedonian Bronze and Early Iron Ages, also played a part in its growth and evolution; a similar influence is also discernible in the Verbicioara culture. The

Coţofeni culture too may have contributed in a small way to the growth of the Tei, since Coţofeni features can be seen in the forms, fabrics and decorative motifs of the Tei pottery. The dwellings of the people belonging to this culture are found on the lower or middle river terraces. Archaeological deposits are not very thick; it was only at a later stage that the 'Zolniki' encampments were found, and these are related to a more developed type of human society. The economy is still of a mixed agricultural-pastoral type, with either agriculture or stock-breeding predominating according to local conditions. Metals are still uncommon, and the number of bronze tools that have been discovered is small; they include a single axe with a crescentic blade having very slightly raised edges, typologically related to examples from the north-east. Other axes, as well as bronze knives or pins called *Hirtenstabnadel,* recovered from the lake-shore site of Tei, place this type at a rather late stage in the Bronze Age. Curved knives, already present in the Glina culture, are found. There was also a bone bridle-bit, similar to those from central and east-central Europe. Pottery *Fig. 41* shows an exceptional variety of shapes and novel decorative motifs. There are coarse jars for storing foodstuffs and water. Vessels of fine ware include cups with a strap-handle, and later, larger vessels with one or two strap-handles become widespread; typologically and chronologically these can be related to similar Verbicioara examples. Several cups of an earlier type have a pointed base and an oblique rim. Pots have richly incrusted *Fig. 40* decoration, the spiral motif being frequently used and developed from previous local elements, although influences coming from the south can also be discerned. The hoard from Perşinari, near Tîrgovişte (including a gold dagger, and several silver axes) and the Mycenaean sword from Roşiorii-de-Vede re- *Fig. 37* present the Tei culture at its zenith.

Five main phases have been distinguished in the development of the Tei culture, which lasted throughout the Middle

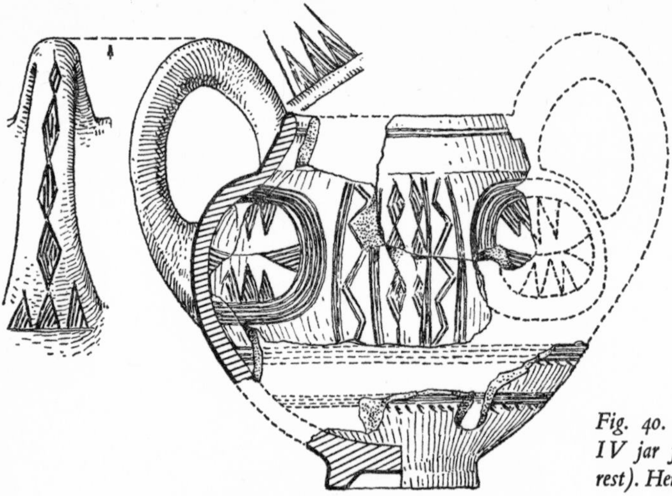

Fig. 40. Decorated Tei phase IV jar from Fundeni (Bucharest). Height, 14.4cm.

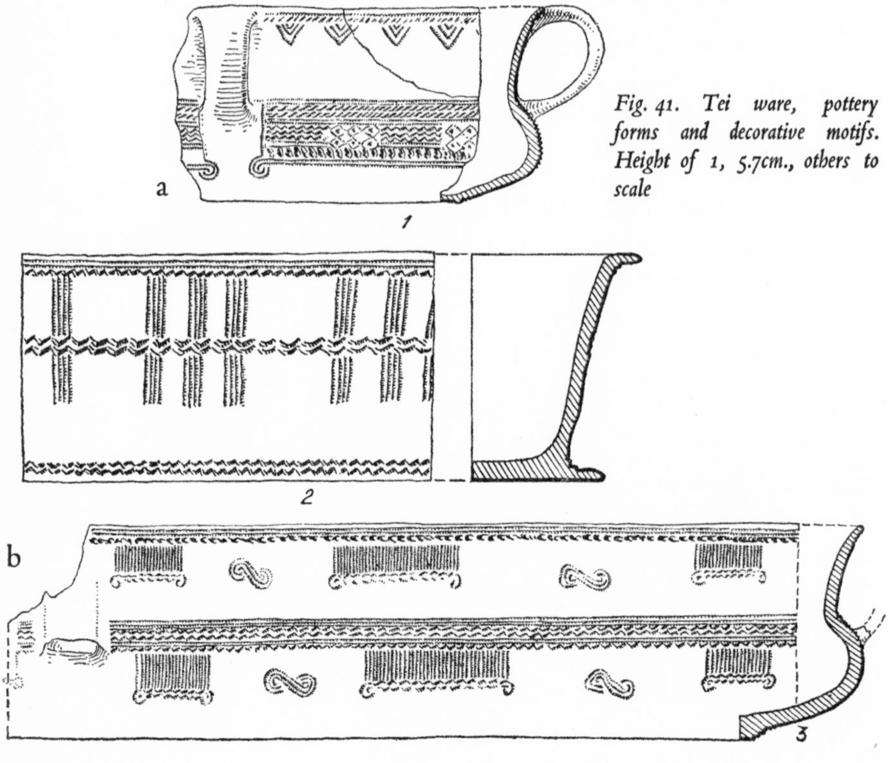

Fig. 41. Tei ware, pottery forms and decorative motifs. Height of 1, 5.7cm., others to scale

and Late Bronze Age and even continued for a time during Bronze IV.

THE VERBICIOARA CULTURE

The zones occupied by the Tei and Verbicioara cultures became very intermingled during the second half of Bronze III, to such an extent that the two styles are almost indistinguishable. It was not until 1949 that it was possible to finally isolate the Verbicioara culture. It covers the whole of Oltenia and spreads also to west Banat, Yugoslavian Banat and the neighbouring regions of Serbia (see the discoveries at Vattina and Kladovo), as well as into north-west Bulgaria (Devetaškata Peštera) or to the east of the Olt. It even penetrated the Carpathians, where caves were sometimes inhabited, as at Baia-de-Fier and Băile Herculane. Settlements of the Verbicioara folk are situated on hill-tops near watercourses, and sometimes fortified with ditches (e.g. the sites at Verbicioara and Sălcuța), or alternatively on the lower river terraces and without any defences. At a later stage, *zolniki* settlements (see p. 83) appear, such as the encampments of Orodel (Oltenia). The economy is still mixed, with either agriculture or stock-breeding predominant. The type-site yielded a considerable number of deer-antler picks, found amongst a deposit of raw materials.

Over most of its area of diffusion in Oltenia the Verbicioara culture can be placed on chronological and stratigraphical grounds between the Glina culture and the first Hallstatt channelled-ware style, and five phases are recognizable.

The archaeological material includes numerous stone, flint, horn and bone tools but bronze objects are exceedingly rare. Curved stone knives are frequent; during phases II and III numerous deer-antler ploughshares indicate increasing agricultural development. Heavy grooved mallets and knobbed mace-heads are also found. Spinning and weaving activities are attested by a considerable number of spindle-whorls of varied and novel form, some of which are even attractively ornamented. A few bronze objects have been recovered, among

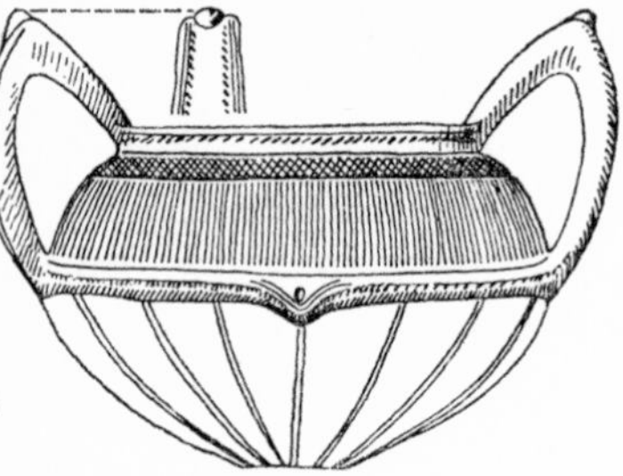

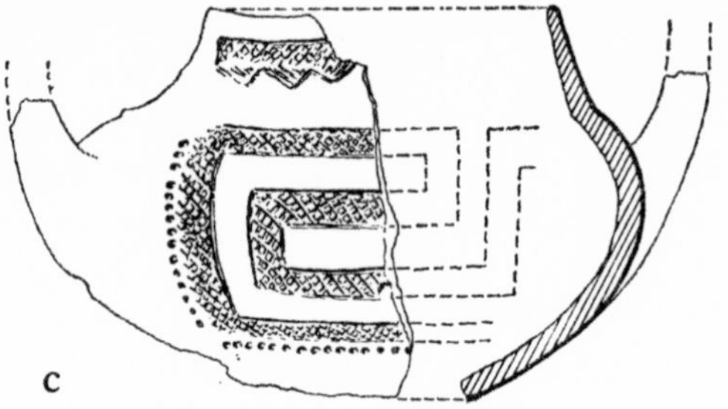

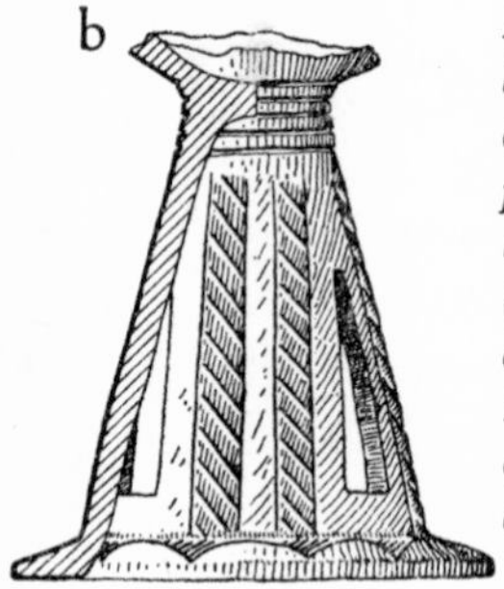

Fig. 42. a, Pot and b, pot stand from Verbicioara, phase IV; c, pottery forms and decoration, of the Tei culture (1), and of the Verbicioara culture, phase V (2). Height of a, 10.4cm.; of b, 14.5cm.; of c, 10 cm. (1), and 15cm. (2)

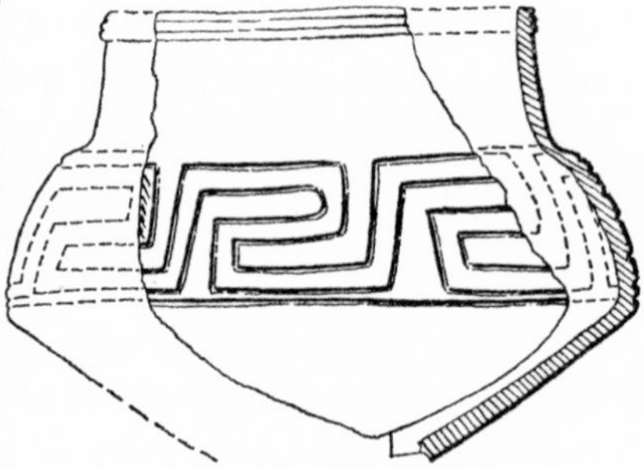

them awls, a 'Cypriot'-type pin and a flat axe with raised edges (of a broad, heavy type).

Fig. 42

Pottery provides the most distinctive element in the material of this culture. It is distinguished primarily by such fine ware, richly ornamented and showing a wide range of forms, as the clepsydra-type vase here reproduced, cups (including the footed variety), bowls, and tiered vases; these recall the Vattina-Gîrla Mare pottery shapes. The vessel or cup with two elegantly curved strap-handles, with trumpet lugs or stylized bird-heads set on the top occurs frequently. Numerous two-handled vessels were discovered in a hoard at Govora-Sat. Found over a wide area, too, is the three-footed bowl, originating in the zone of the Gîrla Mare culture. Decoration is markedly geometric. The spiral is rather rare and the meander appears only during the later phases. At the beginning of this period, the dead were interred, but later, cremated; so far no cemeteries have been discovered. The Verbicioara culture derived from the basic stock of the Periam-Mokrin-Pančevo horizon, as did two other contemporary related cultures: Gîrla Mare and Pecica. The end of the Verbicioara culture is linked to the phenomenon of the 'great Aegean migration' and to the transition to the first Iron Age, when the cultural elements of south and south-west Romania interpenetrated and became merged.

THE GÎRLA MARE CULTURE

This culture, which came into being at the same time as the Verbicioara culture, on the eve of the transition to the Bronze III period, was named after a small island situated near the left bank of the Danube in Oltenia. It should be studied in connexion with the Vattina material. Spreading out on both sides of the Iron Gates, into Vojvodina and north-west Bulgaria (where it penetrates to within 40 km. of Sofia), the Gîrla Mare culture shows certain novel features. Finds of early Verbicioara material have been made in this region, particularly on the Danube and in Banat, but during the later phases the Verbicioara culture developed only to the north of the Gîrla Mare regions. During phases IV and V of the Verbicioara culture, the Gîrla Mare culture deeply penetrated the Verbicioara area and in this way passed into the Tei culture zone. These are continental preliminaries of the 'great Aegean migration', which also involved the proto-Thracian world to the east of the Iron Gates. Growing out of the Periam-Mokrin-Pančevo stock, like the Verbicioara and Pecica cultures, the Gîrla Mare-Vattina culture incorporated a number of heterogeneous elements arising out of the various archaeological levels characteristic of the area of mixed influence around the Iron Gates. It is evident that during its formation a southern element must have been added, in which the spiral and meander pottery decoration played an important part. Only a few settlements

Plate 34

Plate 35

belonging to these people are at present known, and these are located on fairly high river terraces. Many of these sites have been destroyed by flood waters from the Danube, or by drifting sand dunes. No fortified sites have yet been identified. Extensive cemeteries, which are really urn fields, have been found on the left bank of the Danube; some of these have been completely excavated, such as, for example, Cîrna in Oltenia.

An economy based on agriculture led to a more settled way of life, and this in turn had a discernible influence on the material and spiritual development of such communities. It has been suggested that even the persistence of female figurines, which are exceptionally plentiful, is another indication of an agricultural economy, representing agrarian fertility associated with the Mother-Goddess cult. Archaeological evidence shows that a high standard of living was enjoyed by this community; their aesthetic taste can be compared to that of the Mycenaeans, whose influence on people living in this part of Europe cannot be ignored. Stone and bronze weapons (daggers) are relatively rare. Nevertheless the recent discovery (1958) of the Cruceni cemetery in Banat, near the Romanian and Yugoslavian frontier, implies that the bearers of this culture engaged in the warlike activities characteristic of other Bronze Age folk; in this particular cemetry battle-axes with a disked butt, of a Transylvanian type, were found. Daggers and swords had been known for a long time in the vast area covered by the Vattina-Gîrla Mare culture. Bronze and gold ornaments are rare, although some tombs yielded bronze ornaments, such as buckles, bangles and rings. The gold hoard at Țigănași belonged to this culture: it was here that two bangles, several lock-rings and ornaments (*phalerae*) were found in a vase; these most probably represented a tribal hoard, like that at Țufalău or Șmig in Transylvania. The existence of a class structure, which was fully developed by the time of this culture, is indicated by the copious material of some tombs, for example that of a child at

Plate 36

Plate 39

Cruceni where some 20 bronze objects were recovered, or the tombs of cemeteries in Oltenia, with similarly lavish grave goods but only in the form of pottery. The pottery, which is extremely plentiful, is decorated with motifs in which a large part is played by spirals and meanders. There are many different types and shapes of vessels, among them large globular or tiered urns with everted rims, various forms of bowls, cups, jugs and pots, and vessels in the form of birds or with bird-shaped terminals, 'sauce-boats', etc. Other objects were still made of clay, as for example, miniature double-axes, stamps, altars and bell-shaped female figurines. The long evolution of the Gîrla Mare culture covered the entire Middle and Late Bronze Age, and in its latter stages witnessed the gradual transition towards Hallstatt, as did the Pecica culture, which has the same origins.

THE PECICA CULTURE

The Pecica culture spread throughout south-west Romania mainly between the rivers Mureș and Tisa and also in the zone of the Gîrla Mare culture. In my own opinion the old designation of Periam-Pecica should not be retained, since the Periam material and the corresponding levels in Pecica settlements belong to the Early Bronze Age, whereas the Pecica culture develops during Bronze III and IV, like the cultures just referred to and the parallel cultures in south-east Hungary. Metal objects, some of which were worked on the spot, become more numerous; at Pecica, moulds have been found for casting axes with a transverse shaft-hole as well as spearheads and daggers. Faience beads were widely used and, to a certain extent, amber beads also. The bearers of this culture have left gold hoards, similar to those of Gîrla Mare folk, such as the Rovine hoard near Arad.

Pottery is very plentiful; two-handled vessels are in widespread use, while in later phases shapes and ornamentation which could be defined as the 'baroque' style of Pecica ware appear. At this period it is channelled decoration, the *ansa lunata* and the black ware which are most common.

THE MONTEORU CULTURE

In the Monteoru culture, which developed outside the Carpathian region, sites are found mostly on hill-tops where the most easily defended locations were chosen. At a later stage the Monteoru people settled in the plains and on the lower river terraces. One of the highest settlements, the site of 'Cetăţuia' (The City) of Sărata Monteoru, could almost be described as an acropolis and was no doubt an important centre for the tribal community of this region. During the second phase of Monteoru development, an entrenchment was added to this 'Cetăţuia' where it joints the plain, the other steep slopes providing natural defences. Other Monteoru sites similarly fortified are known. Geographical environment favoured stock-breeding, upon which these people mainly subsisted. At its zenith, this culture was characterized by its skilled metal-work; the finished products were included in the trade in faience beads which started in Egypt or in the Helladic or Mycenaean sphere and spread towards central Europe, reaching as far as Great Britain. At Sărata Monteoru a single tomb of a woman provided more than 200 such beads.

Plate 41

The Monteoru culture is a local development of the earlier Glina culture from between the upper Dîmboviţa and the Buzău, which is precisely where the earliest phase of the Monteoru culture is found. From there it spread south towards central Moldavia. Groups of Monteoru people crossed passes in the Carpathians and penetrated into south-east Transylvania. A southern element also contributed to its formation through the Cernavoda culture although it must have passed through the Glina zone. Another element, eastern in origin, can be frequently identified in the archaeological material; finally, in its centre of origin as well as over its area of diffusion, this culture incorporated elements of the final Neolithic and transition periods. In Moldavia this culture overlies the Folteşti horizon, which is, in general, synchronous with the early Glina period. The evolution and development of the Monteoru culture occupied a considerable time. It is possible to identify four main phases in its evolution. The first of these is Monteoru Ia and Ib (respectively I C4 and I C3 according to I. Nestor), which is linked by both its cultural elements and its chronology to early Bronze Age cultures (BII); the second phase in Monteoru II subdivided into a, b, c, d, (=I C2, I C1, Ib and Ia), representing the stage of its final maturing and its expansion towards the north-east, the north and the north-west – the sub-phase Ia being the point of its greatest development and the transition towards the third phase, which is Monteoru III, subdivided into a and b. In this phase, 'Cetățuia' of Sărata Monteoru was fortified with a ditch and production rose sharply, resulting in the improvement of material equipment and a rise in the standard of living as the archaeological evidence suggests. Stone platforms were erected for the dwellings or for the enclosures of the 'sanctuaries', a new improved construction technique for buildings was developed in which stone, wood and daub were used. At Sărata Monteoru evidence was found of parapets with wooden posts and beams. In addition an unusual building-method in the form of 'boxes' made of stone slabs and filled with gravel was employed. Monteoru communities possessed a better social organization based on strong tribal union. Stone, flint and bone tools continued to develop. The similarities between flint arrowheads with types from the north Pontic steppes and the south have been recognized for some considerable time. Among their artifacts were curved stone knives, bronze or bone dagger blades, spearheads, Transylvanian-type battle-axes, moulds for casting axes with transverse shaft-hole, battle-axes made from hard stone and triconic or knobbed mace-heads of the same material. Ornaments are likewise very varied. The following may be mentioned: faience or amber beads, lock-rings of a type generally found in the Carpatho-Danubian area and which developed over a long period, different types of pins, one of which is the *Fig. 43*

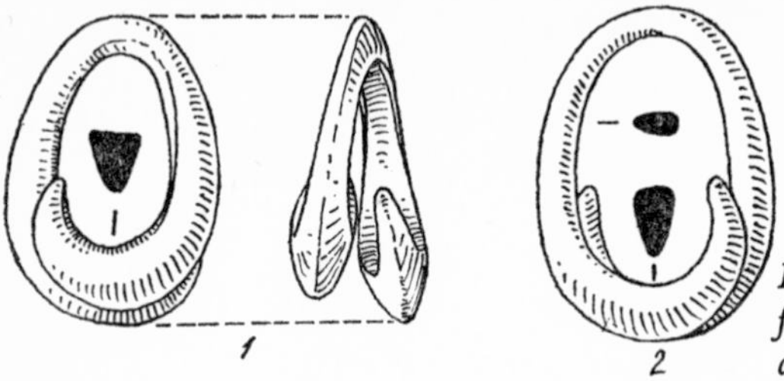

Fig. 43. Lock rings from Sărata Monteoru, found in tomb. Maximum diameter of 1, 2.7 cm., 2 to scale

so-called 'Cypriot' pin, necklaces and pendants. Not to be forgotten are the bone and baked clay *psalia* (bridle-pieces). The pottery has been the subject of close stratigraphical and typological study. The main shapes are: jugs, cups with one or

Fig. 44 two handles, bowls, askoi of southern origin; the novel type

Plate 38 of vessel known as an 'offerings' vase, commonly found in tombs and places of supposed worship (such as the 'sanctuary' at Sărata Monteoru), has a pointed base and a very globular

Plate 40 body with a funnel neck. Handles adopt quite new types and

Fig. 44. Askos *from Poiana, Monteoru culture phase 1a (1c a). Height, 30.5cm.*

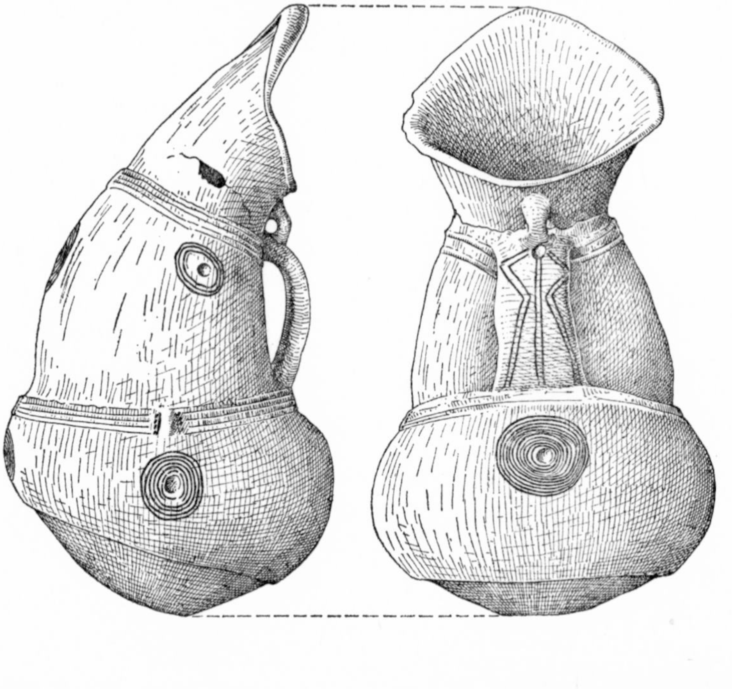

styles such as the *ansa lunata,* which appears at the end of phase II. During phase III the practice of decorating pottery with channels becomes more widespread. The final phase is Monteoru IV, the transition period towards the Noua culture which develops in the same region. Burial is by inhumation in a contracted position, with family groups occupying a single tomb; cremation in urns is attested but on a very small scale. Physically, during the Monteoru period the Mediterranean type is dominant.

Plate 37

Plate 41

THE COSTIŞA CULTURE

To the north of the Monteoru zone a new culture has been identified, which, at Costişa overlies a Monteoru settlement fortified with three ditches. Related to the Bjelyj Potok (Bîlîi Potik) culture, it grew from the heterogeneous stock of the final Neolithic and the transition period; the strong influence of the Monteoru culture can also be seen. Its most distinctive feature is the pottery, among which the shallow bowls belong to the

Plate 45

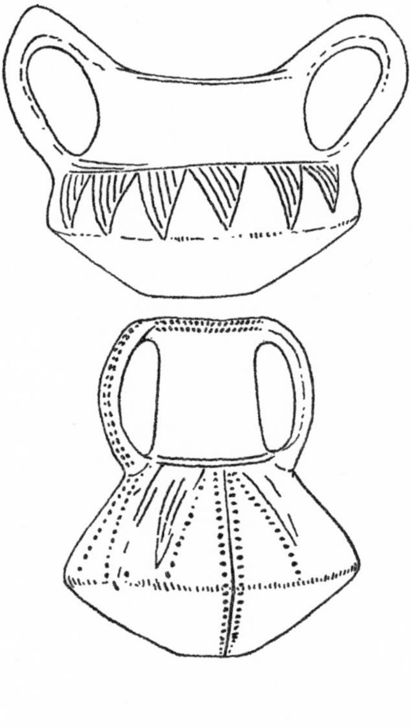

Fig. 45. Pottery from Costişa (Moldavia) Bronze III

earliest phase and attest the presence of elements from the very early Bronze Age in north Moldavia. There are also cups with two lateral strap-handles, jugs and cylindrical-necked amphorae. Decoration assumes a geometric character, the commonest motifs being the hatched triangle and incised lines. This culture played an important part in the formation of the Nordic facies of the Noua culture, and there may also be links with the Komarov assemblage.

THE WIETENBERG CULTURE

When considering the Bronze Age within the arc of the Carpathian range, it should be noted that the cultures east or south of the Carpathians are also diffused in south-east Transylvania, the mountains presenting no barrier.

Bearers of the Wietenberg culture, which occupied a key position in the group of Carpatho-Danubian Bronze Age cultures, were helped in their development by the rich deposits of copper and precious metal ores to be found in this region. Together with the neighbouring tribes of north-east Transylvania, belonging to the Otomani culture, they contributed to the maturing and the increasing prosperity of the Thracian metallurgical industry in central Transylvania. The Wietenberg people built their dwellings on high ground near rivers, or even on hill-tops within the mountainous zone; sometimes they occupied the sites once inhabited by the Coțofeni people.

By 1964, some 200 sites yielding Wietenberg material were known. There are occasional remains of habitation deposits in caves. Though no fortified sites have yet been discovered, the Wietenberg people are unlikely to have been an exception in this respect.

The Wietenberg culture derives mainly from Coțofeni stock, with some heterogeneous elements of the final Neolithic period, and some of the *Furchenstichkeramik* culture. An eastern factor was also assimilated during the formation phase. We cannot determine with any degree of precision the original centre of this culture, but it is certain that in south-east Transylvania – where the Glina culture developed (the Schneckenberg aspect, absent from central Transylvania) – it spread during its second phase, at a time when the Tei and Monteoru groups were being driven back towards the east and south. From existing evidence it would appear that, like the Monteoru and Otomani cultures, the Wietenberg passed through four phases. It continued to evolve, however, until the appearance of the Noua culture, in the same way as did the Monteoru. The Wietenberg people established close relations with other cultures as the diffusion of their products over all the neighbouring areas, and the presence of imports from far afield in the Wietenberg zone, attests. Among the finds were seven Mycenaean swords; and even if these were only local adaptations and not imported articles, it would still confirm the influence of southern elements.

The dwellings are generally surface structures. The Wietenberg site yielded a well-known hearthstone covered with a spiral decoration; there were also curved knives, quite widespread in this culture, stone and bronze axes, flint and bone tools. The relatively large number of stone weapons (spherical and knobbed mace-heads), flanged axes with a knobbed tang, Boiu-type

Fig. 46. a, Baked clay model of a cart from Wietenberg, Wietenberg culture. Height, 9cm. b, Decoration of Wietenberg pottery (after Horedt)

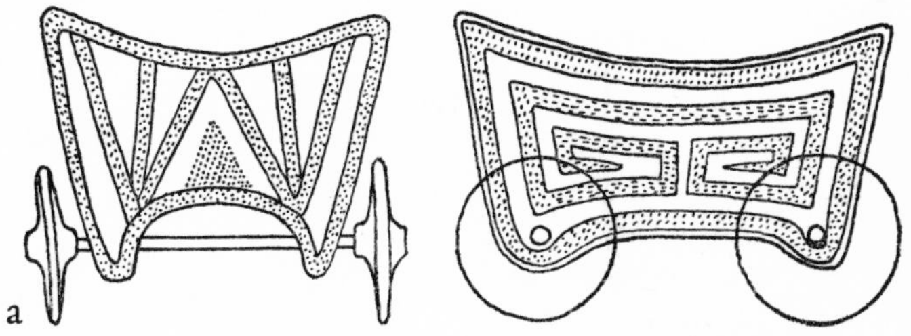

swords, Mycenaean and other types of rapier, as well as the heavy arm-rings discovered in deposits (Ighiel, etc.) denote a markedly warlike attitude. The pottery assumes very distinctive forms and is richly decorated; there are single-handled jugs, bowls of various shapes including the 'square-mouthed' type, footed cups, amphorae, askoi, etc. Two main motifs were used *Fig. 46* for decorating the vessels: the spiral and the meander, yielding various derived and combined designs, particularly at a later phase when the channelled technique first appears. The influence of other cultures as well as the local Carpatho-Danubian stock is reflected in the pottery. Personal ornaments include pins of the 'husk-headed' type (related to the well-known type from a tomb at Vrșac, belonging to the Vattina-Gîrla Mare culture), and those known as disk-headed pins, as well as beads, bangles, etc. Bone *psalia* have also been found.

Burial was both by inhumation and by cremation in urns, as at the Bistrița cemetery (excavated in 1958, and which revealed 38 cremation tombs). At Pianul de Jos (in the Sebeș district) a Wietenberg cemetery was discovered in 1963 providing evidence of both rites. By virtue of its geographical position and the exceptional wealth and diversity of its products, the Wietenberg culture was one of the strongest and most enduring in central Transylvania, contributing in large measure to the formation of the first Iron Age.

THE OTOMANI CULTURE

While the above-mentioned cultures were developing, the Otomani matured in north-west Romania, north-east Hungary and eastern Slovakia, thus creating a link with both central Europe and the Pecica-Vattina-Gîrla Mare and Wietenberg cultures. It was not an eastern variation of the elements from east Hungary; as a culture it arose within its own zone situated between the Apuseni mountains, the Lower Mureș and the Tisa. It is here that it began its evolution, incorporating elements of the Baden, *Furchenstichkeramik* culture, of the tumulus culture of east Slovakia, of the mixed 'eastern' horizon and the persisting Bronze Age Vučedol elements. This same autochthonous origin is attested by research in Slovakia, in particular at the fortified site and cemetery of Barca, near Košice. Sites attributable to Otomani people are set on high ground fortified with ditches and earth ramparts, like the 'Cetățuia' of Otomani or the Barca settlement. The second type of site is that described as 'atoll-shaped', where the dwellings are concentrically arranged, as at the Otomani settlement (in the locality of 'Cetatea de Pămînt'), and Vărșand, at Socodor and in several other places. These fortifications have no earth ramparts. The third and more frequent type of settlement is that found on river terraces with no added fortifications. The bearers of this culture lived in spacious houses with one, two or even three rooms, such as those at Barca. Dwellings were quadrangular and sometimes surprisingly large; at Otomani one house was found to measure 24½ m. by 12½. Metal-working was developed and intensified by the Otomani groups, thanks to the rich copper ores found on the spot and the ease with which they could obtain the necessary tin from neighbouring regions. This was the area where the production of bronze equipment reached its highest level and where distinctive types of weapon such as the widely used Thracian battle-axes were fashioned; and in this same zone large numbers of swords, daggers and wrist-guards were produced. Numerous bronze and gold objects have been recovered from the sites and tombs. The pottery assumes novel shapes, among them cups and jugs with handles, and shallow dishes and bowls. Decoration takes the form of spiral motifs, bands, incised lines, concentric circles and channels, these being usually associated with conical warts around which they are often arranged.

The Otomani culture was in close contact with other Bronze III cultures. Fairly numerous finds of bone *psalia*, at Otomani, Socodor and Vărșand, similar to the Hungarian models, suggest that the horse was being used.

As in Slovakia and Hungary, both inhumation and cremation were practised by the Otomani people of Romania (Ciumești, Pir, Valea lui Mihai, etc.). Osteological studies carried out in the Pir cemetery have established the predominance among these people of a brachycephalic type, with a slight trace of Alpine influence.

In the Carpatho-Danubian area of its diffusion the Otomani culture acted as the leaven which later gave rise to the Hallstatt horizon. Recent research indicates that the Suciu culture resulted from a fusion of the Otomani group with southern elements of Pecica-Vattina origin and others (*e.g.* Wietenberg) coming from the south-east.

HOARDS AND TREASURES

Fig. 47

During the long Carpatho-Danubian Bronze Age, a number of gold and bronze objects were produced within the local culture groups; certain of these, described above, were diffused throughout the entire Carpatho-Danubian region and even beyond. Although gold ornaments existed as early as the Late Neolithic, it was only during the Bronze Age that, like bronze objects, they became more widely used.

Horizon A This first horizon belongs to the Bronze II phase, as evidenced, for example, by the series of hoards found at Ostrovul Corbului, Baniabic (Vîlcele), Porava, and elsewhere; the Perșinari treasure and the Tufa hoard belong to the period of transition from phase B IIb to phase B IIIa (about 1600 BC).

Horizon B The second horizon pertains to the Bronze IIIa phase (1600–1500 BC), when important metallurgical centres were already in existence in the Carpathian region. One of the most representative hoards of this first series is that of Apa (Transylvania) which includes the following objects: a sword with a solid hilt; another sword belonging to the same type but

Plates 31–33

with a disk-pommel; a battle-axe with a disk which has a small 'umbo' or stud; an axe with an elongated crescent-shaped butt; a boat-axe with a disk, and also a heavy arm-ring. The

Chronology		Phases	Reinecke	H. Müller-Karpe	Horizon	Hoards
EARLY BRONZE AGE	1700	IIb	A		A	Schitu, Ostrovu Corbului Baniabic, Borleşti, Parava etc.
	1600					Perşinari, Tufa
MIDDLE AND LATE BRONZE AGE		IIIa	B		B	Apa, Ţufalău, Şmig etc.
	1500	IIIb	C_1		C	Ighiel, Turda, Iclod, Pecica etc.
	1400	IIIc	C_2		D	Vărşand, Otomani
FINAL BRONZE AGE AND TRANSITION	1300	IV a b	D	XIIIc.	E	Uriu, Domăneşti, Drajna de Jos, Ulmi, Ilişeni, Nicolae Bălcescu, etc.
EARLY IRON AGE	1200	I a b	A_1	XIIc.	F	Uioara, Cincu, Suseni, Pecica (Ha I_a) etc.
	1100					

Fig. 47. Tentative chronology and classification of the Bronze Age hoards in Romania

distinctive form of both swords and their rich decoration, as well as the typological classification of other objects and their association with datable material in other hoards or sites have, in recent years, enabled a more precise date to be given to the horizon B treasures and hoards. Moreover, the type of axe found at Apa and Ţufalău, as well as the earlier series of gold lock-rings and ornaments (*phalerae*) from treasures such as those of Ţufalău, Ţigănaşi, Şmig, Grăniceri, Otlaca, etc. – which can be paralleled either in the early Mycenaean world of the shaft-grave period or at Naumburg, in the north European Bronze Age as recorded from Romanian stratigraphical evidence – together suggest that the hoard and treasure horizon at Apa-Ţufalău can be definitely attributed to a Bronze IIIa date – that is, about 1600 BC. The Bronze IIIa phase represents, in all the local Bronze Age cultures, a period of growth and diffusion of bronze metallurgy and gold-working, implying that these warrior-people had a particular liking for personal ornaments. The Thracian tribal aristocracy, who were at this time leading a life of luxury and well-being, combined a taste for personal ornaments with their need for weapons with which to carry on their warlike activities. Certain weapons were in fact for show only or constituted a symbol of wealth; this is clearly illustrated by one of the five axes from Ţufalău weighing only 485.92 grams. In the same treasure there were, among the axes, eight examples of *phalerae* richly ornamented with spirals, as well as a quantity of unworked gold. The Şmig treasure contained a necklace or chain made of 17 gold rings, 26 decorated *phalerae*, 5 silver beads, a number of gold beads, a bangle and some unworked gold. The presence of the last-named implies that there were workshops specializing in gold-working, the goldsmith's craft developing alongside the metallurgical industries. It is particularly interesting that the bronze and gold objects were distributed throughout the entire area covered by the Bronze Age cultures. To the treasures of the Carpathian region, which have been known for some time, must be added that of Ţigănaşi, on the Danube (in Oltenia), in an area densely inhabited by Gîrla Mare people. This treasure consisted of 50 gold objects (of which 33 were *phalerae*) deposited in a vessel of Gîrla Mare ware. Other gold objects have been found on the sites or recovered from the tombs; while yet others were chance finds.

Plate 39

The bronze and gold objects of this horizon, which come from all over the Carpatho-Danubian region as a result of their widespread diffusion through intertribal exchanges, recall, by their ornamentation, the decorated ware of the local cultures (Tei, Gîrla Mare, Pecica, Wietenberg, Otomani, etc.); Mycenaean influence can also be seen, for example, in the way it affected the design and decoration of *phalerae*. It was in fact the Mycenaean civilization that helped the local cultures to ad-

Plate 39

vance, hurrying them towards the transition from the Bronze II to the following Bronze III phase.

Cultural Continuity The development of Bronze Age cultures was not interrupted when the Bronze III phase succeeded phase II; the basic shapes and decoration of their pottery, the products of the metallurgical workshops and of the goldsmiths' shops continued to improve noticeably; thus, earlier types are seen associated with novel forms, distinctive of Bronze IIIb (1500–1400, or C_1). This continuity can be clearly seen in the series of Thracian battle-axes; certain elements, such as the shaft-hole and the point are added but the essential form of the axe remains unchanged. One of these new types, exemplified by an axe from Ighiel, near Alba-Iulia, is associated with an earlier type (without a shaft hole). Boiu-type swords are widely distributed and show affinities with the Italian examples. Long-headed axes, sickles, bangles, crescentic or heart-shaped pendants, various types of hair-pins and gold ornaments (rings, bangles, etc.) continue to be made.

Horizon C Chronologically and historically it is Horizon C of the hoards and treasures which constitutes the Bronze IIIb phase.

The Bronze IIIc phase (1400–1300, or C_2) brought no break in the activities of the metallurgical workshops and goldsmiths' shops. It is noticeable that with the advent of Bronze III, tools not only begin to appear in the hoards but also become more numerous in other sites, where casting moulds are found, as for example at Sărata Monteoru and Pecica. This tendency continues during the Bronze IIIc phase, represented by Horizon D of the metal hoards. Recent Romanian research into hoards has shown that, during the late and final Bronze Age, novel types of tools and weapons were produced, which appear in the Bronze IV Horizon E and during the Hallstatt Ia (horizon F).

Chapter VI

The Late Bronze and Early Iron Ages

THE FINAL PHASE (B IV)

THE TRANSITION from the magnificent Thracian Bronze Age cultures to the Iron Age occurred gradually and systematically without any real interruption or break. Recent archaeological research carried out in Romania completely invalidates the theory that the Bronze Age cultures were abruptly cut short by the sudden arrival of a new culture the rise and diffusion of which was largely due to the Cimmerians and the Scythians.

Towards the end of the Bronze Age, large-scale interpenetrations and combinations of tribes and their various cultures took place in east-central and south-east Europe, and led quite naturally to cultural, ethnical and biological assimilations. This process, which had begun during the final phase of the Bronze Age, resulted in mixed cultures or very large cultural groups. It is represented in certain instances by Horizon V, and it was at this stage that the foundations of the Iron Age were laid. The Verbicioara, Gîrla Mare and Tei cultures were among those that thus interpenetrated and cohered, with the result that they formed a vast aggregation with similar, even identical features. This applies to the texture, shapes and decoration of the pottery and reflects the changing way of life of these tribes. The earlier type of encampment is, however, still found. Large double vases with a wide strap-handle are distributed throughout the Muntenian plain and the Danube valley; for example, the vase found at Orlea, near the town of Corabia, and another belonging to a later phase in the Vîrtop culture. This type of vessel, already in existence during the Middle,

Bronze Age in the area of the Gîrla Mare-Verbicioara cultures and found in the Hallstatt IIa horizon of the Vîrtop assemblage, provides the best evidence of continuity and of the relationship between the local Bronze Age cultures and their Early Iron Age counterparts. Amongst the material of this same culture are the footed cup (which possesses a distinct functional aspect), the winged vase, and, of course, the later type of 'Villanovan' biconical urn.

Finds made in Banat, Oltenia and Muntenia of material belonging to the fifth and last Bronze Age phase in these areas, have provided the very first continental evidence of 'the great Aegean migration' which developed along a wide front extending from east of the Iron Gates to the mouth of the Olt and the valley of the Lower Danube. This is attested by the Danubian elements – pottery shapes, decorative motifs such as the meander, figurine types, etc. – which are found in Macedonia and Greece. Recently, this heterogeneous horizon V has also been identified in Dobrudja, although only by isolated finds. A recently established fact is the extent to which the Wietenberg, Otomani and Pecica cultures interpenetrated and fused in the north-west (paralleling what was happening south of the Carpathians), thereby giving rise to the Suciu culture (Maramureș).

THE SUCIU CULTURE

This also spread to the neighbouring regions of Hungary and is synchronous with Horizon V south of the Carpathians and the Noua culture in Moldavia and Transylvania. Cremation was practised by its bearers, who used urns covered by a lid (of pottery or stone slabs). The novel and distinctive pottery includes vessels with a strap-handle and geometric decoration – triangles, circles, zig-zag lines and spirals – excised and incrusted with white paste. The large knobs on these vases have a decorative design around them.

Fig. 48

Fig. 50

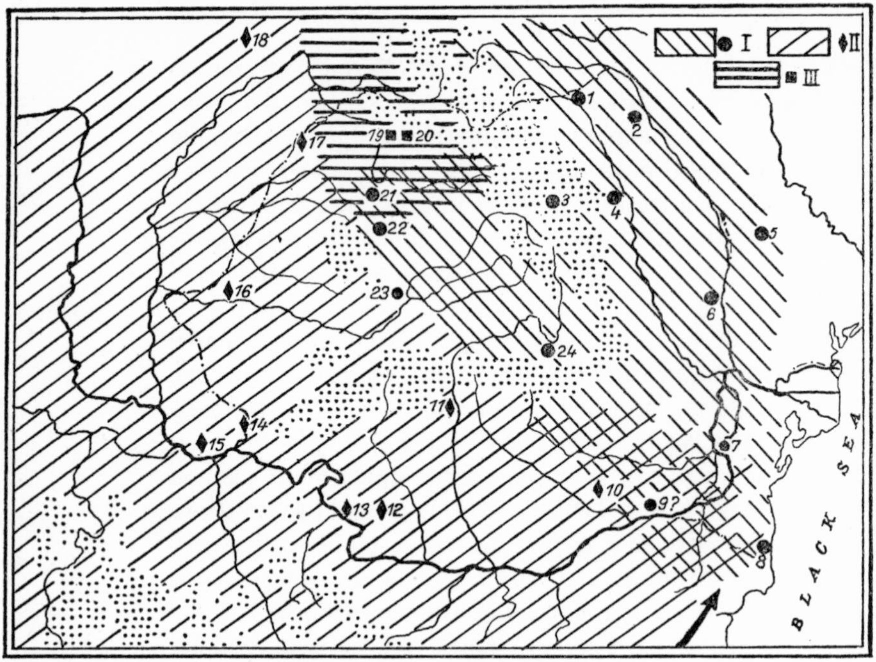

Fig. 48. The final Bronze Age and transition to the Iron Age in Romania

I Noua culture; II Horizon V; III Suciu de Sus culture

1 Vlădeni
2 Truşeşti
3 Piatra Neamţ
4 Holboca
5 Grădiştea
6 Cavadineşti
7 Hîrşova (?)
8 Limanu (?)
9 Dorobanţu
10 Bucharest
11 Vlădeşti
12 Verbicioara
13 Gîrla Mare
14 Vattina
15 Dubovac
16 Pecica
17 Otomani
18 Barca
19 Lăpuş
20 Suciu de Sus
21 Hida
22 Gilău
23 Teiuş
24 Braşov-Noua

THE NOUA CULTURE

While in Banat and south of the Carpathians the mixed horizon V developed, and in the neighbouring areas the Suciu assemblage, the Noua culture came into being in Moldavia, north-east Muntenia and central Transylvania. In these regions it provided a stepping-stone to the Hallstatt cultures. It can be dated to the last phase of the Bronze Age and the transition period leading to the Iron Age, overlying deposits of the Monteoru culture (final phase); it is, in turn, covered by the earliest Hallstatt channelled-ware horizon (Hallstatt Ia). Branches of the Noua culture extend eastwards into the Moldavian S.S.R. and northwards into the Sub-Carpathian region of the Ukrainian S.S.R. Its western boundary is marked by the Apuseni mountains. Plate 45

Noua sites, identified only during the last two decades, are unfortified; they are encampments which contain in the archaeological levels a large quantity of ashes (*zolniki*). Numerous bones of domestic animals in the deposits indicate an intensification of stock-breeding, agriculture occupying only a secondary place at this time, although sites have also yielded very large querns. Hunting activities still contributed to subsistence. From the site of Cavadinești in Moldavia the bone side-pieces (*psalia*) of a horse bit were recovered. Archaeological material from huts, which are the prevalent type of dwelling, is scanty; it consists of bone objects (arrowheads, needles, sickles, notched animal shoulder-blades, etc.), and bronze bangles, pins and *Fig. 49* several sickles. Pottery includes cups with one or two strap- Plate 50 handles, some with conical warts or ridges, bowls and storage jars. Decoration is limited to applied bands with indentations, incised lines and occasional grooves. The cemeteries of Transylvania (Noua, Morești, Cluj, Teiuș, Alba-Iulia, etc.) and Moldavia (Trușești, Piatra-Neamț, Probota, etc.), show that inhumation was the rule; there is less evidence of cremation. The Noua culture has a unified structure though there are certain distinctive local elements, and three phases are recognizable. The first phase corresponds with the Va Horizon and is *Fig. 50* synchronous with the Suciu culture. In some places – particularly east of the Carpathians – this period persisted until the Hallstatt culture finally emerged. The importance of the Noua

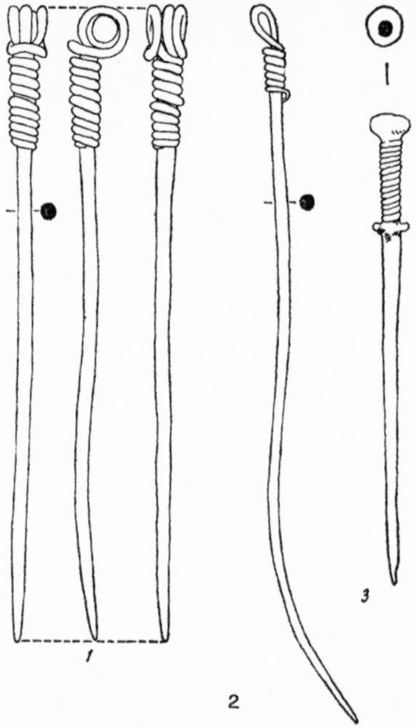

Fig. 49. Pins of the Noua culture. 1, 2, of the Cypriot type from Gîrbovăţ (Moldavia); 3, knob-headed type from Teiuş (Transylvania). Length of 1, 16.5 cm., others to scale

culture is that, in the area of its diffusion, it preserved the traditions of the Thracian Bronze Age cultures and handed them down to the first Iron Age. It has extensive links, particularly with the Sabatinovka culture, the distinctive Srubnaya Grave group, and the regions of south and south-west Europe. Anthropologically speaking, the Noua people do not constitute

Fig. 50. Suciu de Sus pottery. Height of 3, 11.5cm., others to scale

a homogeneous group: in Transylvania brachycephalic types have been recorded, while in Moldavia dolichocephalic and mesocephalic elements predominate.

HORIZON E OF THE BRONZE HOARDS

During the period that witnessed the end of the Bronze Age and the development of the Noua culture, bronze metallurgy made quite exceptional progress in the Carpatho-Danubian region. At the same time stock-breeding became more important. Bronze hoards attributable to Reinecke's period D (thirteenth century BC) belong to the horizon or series known as Uriu-Domănești. Objects found in the hoards include a variety of tools (studded, hooked or tanged sickles, axes and celts), weapons (the later type of Thracian disked and studded battle-axe) or assorted ornaments (hammer-pins, fibulae, bracelets, etc.). Similar hoards have been reported in Dobrudja during the last five years, as for example the one discovered in the village of Nicolae Balcescu; this would imply that intense metallurgical activities were carried on in that region of Romania situated between the Danube and the Black Sea, and most probably in contact with the flourishing Transylvanian centres. Recent finds once again confirm that the Carpathians and the Danube have never constituted a barrier to the spread of cultures. Hoards from Drajna de Jos (Muntenia), Ilișeni and Liteni (Moldavia) may be attributed to the Noua culture, the Suciu culture or to Horizon V of the Bronze Age cultures.

Fig. 47

CHAPTER VII

The First Iron Age: Hallstatt

THE GENERAL SCENE

THE IRON AGE began at a time when general conditions were already totally different from those which had existed during the Bronze Age. Economic life becomes mainly pas-toral in character, as works of art and ritual practices suggest; stock-breeding is the predominant occupation, cultivation pro-viding only subsidiary food supplies. Certain ritual practices are partially or totally abandoned. Settlements become more densely populated and their number increases – there is no question of either depopulation or the arrival of new com-munities from outside. Climatic changes play their part in de-termining the new way of life. Fortified sites, with banks and ditches (Mediaș, Teleac, Sîntana, Lăpuș), still exist. The rate of social and economic advance does not follow the same pat-tern in all tribes or tribal groups, and about the middle of the first millennium BC these differences become more marked. One of the main reasons for this inequality was the close relationship with the Mediterranean civilization, which became even more important after the foundation of the Greek colonies on the west coast of the Black Sea. The predominantly pastoral eco-nomy which was developing throughout central Europe during the first Iron Age, as well as the intense activity of the bronze workshops and foundries, led to increasingly frequent inter-tribal exchanges; this in itself brought about changes in the structure of the tribal aristocracy composed of warriors who had become wealthy as a result of these exchanges. Remains of chariots and parts of harness show that the horse was used soon after 800 BC both for horse-drawn chariots and as a mount. It is in fact during the final phase of the Bronze Age, the transi-tion period and the early part of the Hallstatt period that the

Fig. 51

Plate 49

Chronology		Phases		Reinecke	H. Müller-Karpe	South-Thracian Zone	North-Thracian Zone
Early Hallstatt	1200	I	a	A_1	XII c.	Babadag $I_{a,b}$	Noua III, Suciu de Sus, Lăpuș
	1100					Pecica	Sîntana
			b	A_2	XI c.	Babadag II	Reci
	1000	II	a	B_1	X c.	Balta Verde (Urnfield)	Mediaș
	900					Vîrtop	Vîrtop
			b	B_2	IX c.		
	800					Proto-Basarabi	Proto-Basarabi
Middle Hallstatt		III	a	B_3	VIII c.	Basarabi	Basarabi
	700		b	C		Balta Verde	Stoicani
Late and Final Hallstatt	600					Ferigile – Bîrsești	
	550	IV	a	D_1			
	500						
	450		b	D_2		Earliest and Early La Tène	Late and Latest Hallstatt
	400		c	D_3			
	300						

Fig. 51. Tentative chronology of the Early Iron Age (Hallstatt) in Romania

sword and the battle-axe were most widely diffused. In west and south-west Romania, a number of different weapons come from the Hallstatt Illyrian workshops of the north-west Balkans. Burial was both by cremation and by inhumation.

CHRONOLOGY

The general problems of relative and absolute chronology have now been resolved and the various phases of evolution of the first Iron Age in Romania determined. Stratigraphical evidence has confirmed that the Hallstatt channelled-ware horizon overlies the Noua archaeological level or the final Wietenberg, Verbicioara and Gîrla Mare cultural layers, its upper limit being marked by the appearance of Greek imports, and of Scythian, south Thracian and Celtic elements. The Hallstatt period came to an end at different times in the various areas of Romania: in Dobrudja and the Danubian-Pontic zone it ended about 450 BC, in the rest of the country about 300 BC. Where the beginnings of the Iron Age are concerned, finds of Peschiera-type fibulae at Cernatu (Transylvania), Jupa (Banat), Orlea and Horezu (in a hoard) in Oltenia, are of particular interest, since the earliest example of this type can be dated to about 1200 to 1150 BC. Thus the first Iron Age may be assumed to have begun, in some areas of Romania at least, around 1200 BC.

THE ORIGINS AND FORMATION OF THE HALLSTATT CULTURES

The intense activity of bronze foundries and workshops during the transition stage from Bronze to Iron Age, caused novel types of weapons, tools, vessels and ornaments to circulate, the old Bronze V forms assuming a new appearance in Hallstatt I. Where did the formation of Hallstatt cultures first start? Our present state of knowledge leads us to believe that there were three different regions from which the changes stemmed, namely: Dobrudja; a second centre somewhere in south-west and west Romania; and, finally, the north-west region, which includes north-east Hungary and east Slovakia. There is reason to believe that, of these, Dobrudja can lay claim to be the place or origin of the earliest Hallstatt horizon. During the initial Hallstatt period the bearers of the Pecica-Gîrla Mare-Dubovac cultures played an active part. This was responsible for spreading the technique of the black channelled ware, the biconical urn and the 'turban'-shaped bowl, in Transylvania and the neighbouring regions. Furthermore it is conceivable that events in the north-west Balkans, the eastern zone of the Alps and in the lower basin of the Tisa (Tumulus Bronze culture) also contributed to the formation of the Hallstatt culture. It is now certain that the transition to the Hallstatt cultures resulted from intense and differentiated local development, representing a further significant step in the cultural advance of the Romanian peoples.

THE SPREAD OF IRON METALLURGY

Iron was used by the indigenous population at least as early as Hallstatt II (b). The bronze hoard at Hida (Transylvania) datable to Ha IIa or IIb yielded, in addition to the bronze socketed axes, tanged sickles and spearheads, a knife with a bronze antennae hilt in which were still preserved fragments of an iron blade. During excavations carried out in 1963 at Babadag, a pointed iron bar and two pieces of iron were recovered from a level attributable to Ha II. The presence of this new metal in Dobrudja found in a context dated with certainty to the second Hallstatt period, most probably IIa, throws light on the distribution of iron in the Lower Danube area. As far as is known, the spread of technological knowledge concerning ironworking began after the destruction of the Hittite empire, during the 'great Aegean migration'. This 'technological revolution' penetrated south-east and central Europe by a number of different routes. One of these began in Anatolia, crossed Greece, the Balkans and central Europe and finally reached the Carpatho-Danubian zone. Account should also be taken of certain tributaries which branch off from the main line of penetration, such as that which ran from the east Balkans towards the Dobrudja region. Another route, which was actively used over a long period and may be termed the Cimmerian route (associated as it was with elements of the 'Thraco-Cimmerian', or 'Cimmero-Agathyrisian', historical horizon), started in the

Caucasus and followed the steppes north of the Black Sea. All these routes – and there were others, including the Italian route – were in general synchronous and convergent.

EARLY HALLSTATT I AND II

Ha I and II cover the period from 1200 to 800 BC, and one of the two zones in which the first Hallstatt elements are attested is that comprising south-west Romania, Serbia and south-east Hungary, an area covered by the great Vattina-Gîrla Mare-Pecica-Dubovac culture, from which the Tumulus Bronze culture influence had come. Occupation sites and tombs have yielded blackish-brown pottery decorated with slanting grooves or parallel fluted lines arranged obliquely, in arch-designs or in vertical or horizontal groups. Occasionally the channelling surrounds protuberances on the vase which have been slipped and polished to give them a metallic shine.

THE FIRST CHANNELLED WARE

The main type of vase found is the so-called 'Villanovan Urn', like the representative example from Pecica, which contained a hoard datable to Ha Ia. Some models resemble the 'tiered' vases. 'Torque'-impressed and white incrusted designs were employed for ornamentation. The spiral motif is still used to decorate vases. This channelled-ware, or Pecica, horizon can be dated by the Peschiera-type fibula.

THE SÎNTANA-LĂPUȘ HORIZON

The Ha Ia period saw the simultaneous development in Crișana and Maramureș of a channelled-ware horizon which included artifacts of the Hungarian Gava culture. Excavations at the fortified site of Sîntana (Crișana) and in the Lăpuș (Maramureș) mound yielded characteristic burnished channelled ware, the most distinctive shape being the vessel with large conical protuberances surrounded by parallel channelling. Certain elements of the Ha Ia horizon anticipate the Basarabi culture and the so-called 'Thraco-Cimmerian' horizon of Hallstatt III. The shapes of some of the pottery vessels and even the gold vases (those from Vîlcitrîn in Bulgaria, for instance) show this, as do the technique employed for decoration and the motifs used. The dead were cremated.

The Pecica horizon (Ha Ia) is attested by archaeological evidence in central and south-east Transylvania, and at Reci. This horizon appears east of the Carpathians in Moldavia during the Ha Ib phase, and it would seem that phase III of the Noua culture did not die out in this region until after the beginning of the Hallstatt. Plate 47

Babadag I In recent years fortified Hallstatt sites have been discovered in Dobrudja, such as the one at Babadag, which, with its ditches and earth rampart, is a veritable early Thracian *oppidum.* The archaeological deposit occupies six levels; the black burnished pottery has grooves or fluting. Large sherds belonging to biconical vessels are decorated with protuberances surrounded by grooves, while circles associated with tangential lines decorate other potsherds. There are also 'turban'-shaped bowls. This cultural facies was diffused throughout south-east Muntenia and south Moldavia. Archaeological material showing affinities with these elements was unexpectedly found in the Jassy district. Here, a cremation tomb, at Trifeşti, produced pottery which in form and decoration resembled the more evolved types of Babadag ware; at the same time, these finds can be related to those made at Mediaş. Plate 45

Ha Ib Urnfields In a Hallstatt urnfield at Balta Verde were found 'Villanovan' funerary urns with bowl-shaped lids. The decoration on pottery consists of grooves, sometimes in arch-shaped designs, or of oblique and parallel facets; this horizon is derived from the Pecica (Ha Ia) horizon.

THE SECOND CHANNELLED WARE

In Oltenia one cultural group of the early Hallstatt period is known as Vîrtop, corresponding in Transylvania to a rich layer in the Hallstatt deposit at Mediaş and the finds at Lechinţa which have analogies with the Vál-Dálj culture. This is represented by settlements in the form of rather flattened *tells*, Plates 48-50, 52 Plate 46

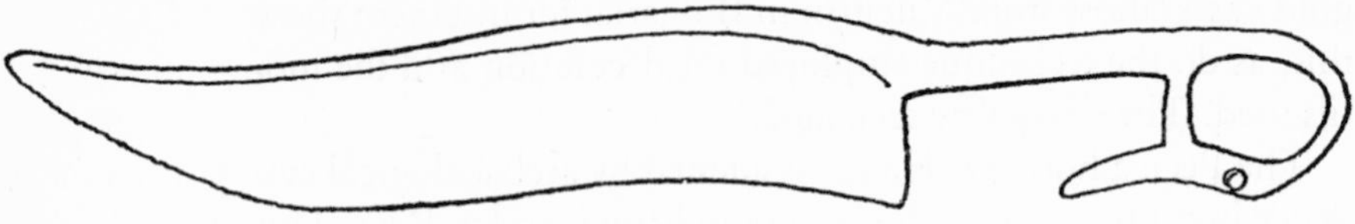

Fig. 52. Knife with a birdhead handle from the Şpălnaca hoard

with only a thin cultural level, occasionally appearing as de-posits (*zolniki*). The dead were cremated and buried under a barrow; grave furniture includes double-vases, winged vases and vessels on a perforated pedestal typical of the Vattina-Gîrla Mare-Dubovac tradition. Material attributable to this horizon has also been found at Oinac (Muntenia). At this time the Babadag culture continues to develop, while in Transylvania, the fortified site at Mediaş and, in part, that of Drîmbar-Teleac, throw some light on life in the Ha II period.

HORIZON F OF THE HOARDS

The Ha Ia period is attested by an exceptionally large number of hoards and hoard-foundries; and these contain a considerable quantity of objects and raw material sometimes reaching an over-all weight which, for the period, is impressive; The Uioara hoard, for example, contained 5,800 pieces – including 'scrap-iron' – weighing 1300 kg. all told. To this same series may be added the hoards at Spălnaca, Pecica, Cincu, Suseni (all in Transylvania), Oinac (in Muntenia), and Poarta Albă (in Dobrudja) – the latter including two pieces of gold foil worked in *repoussé* and folded into a cylindrical shape.

Fig. 52, Plate 43

Plate 42

Recent discoveries in Dobrudja have confirmed that, during the initial Hallstatt period, a prosperous and novel bronze-metallurgy was developing in this area, the products of which show affinities with articles from the important Transylvanian foundries and the Moldavian hoards. It shows that in general the workshops and foundries developed in unison and went on working during the Ha IIa, Ha IIb and Ha III periods. At this time bronze-metallurgy showed intense activity, using all the available local resources, and took advantage of various inter-tribal exchanges. Stock-breeding as well as the mining of salt and gold became increasingly important. The warlike character of the people at this time is indicated by the number of weapons, such as Pecica-type swords, helmets, etc. Numerous agricultural implements were, however, found and the apparent liking for personal ornament is revealed by the many bronze ornaments often delicately worked.

HORIZON G-I OF THE HOARDS

Production continues along the same lines as before and workshops show intensified activity during these stages; implements, particularly axe/adzes and bronze sickles, increase in number; arm-bands persist; similar types are to be found on both sides of the Carpathians. The most representative hoards are those at Moigrad, Tăuteu and Oradea (with gold objects).

The sword with a cup-shaped pommel surmounting the hilt, a type found at Cobor, belongs to the Hallstatt IIa period. The Ha IIb period saw the spread of antennae swords (e.g. the Bunești sword) and spectacle-fibulae. Among the more notable hoards are those found at Fizeșul Gherlei, Gușterița, Hida and Singeorgiu-de-Pădure. *Fig. 53* *Fig. 54*

The Basarabi Culture This developed at the end of the early Hallstatt period and during the transition to Hallstatt III. At this time, in contrast to the generally uniform Hallstatt horizon, a process of integration and unification of the earlier traditions, against a background of north Thracian stock, is discernible, a process which, from the chronological point of view, occurs throughout Romanian Territory and even spreads to other areas. *Fig. 56*

Sites, in which local bronze traditions persist, take the form of encampments detectable by the ash-deposits (*zolniki*); there are also some dispersed settlements. These sites contain huts, hearths, silos and ritual pits. A pit of this kind was excavated at Verbița, and near the heap of earth removed when the pit was dug were traces of fire(charcoal, ashes), animal bones and

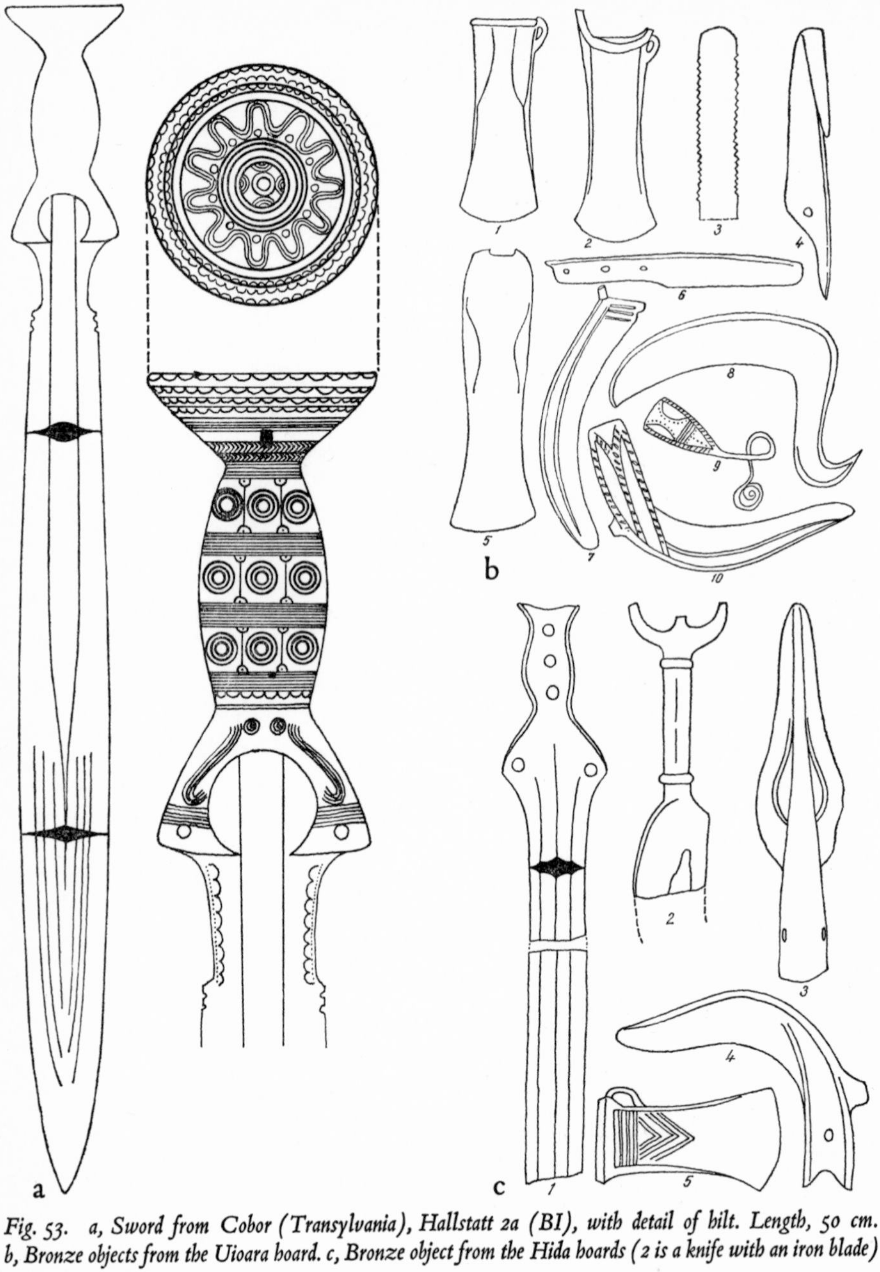

Fig. 53. a, Sword from Cobor (Transylvania), Hallstatt 2a (BI), with detail of hilt. Length, 50 cm. b, Bronze objects from the Uioara hoard. c, Bronze object from the Hida hoards (2 is a knife with an iron blade)

Chronology: Relative	Chronology: Date	Phases		Hoards	Horizon	Reinecke	H. Müller-Karpe
EARLY HALLSTATT	1200–1100	I	a	Uioara, Cincu, Oinac, Suseni, Pecica, Poarta Albă etc.	F	A_1	XII c.
EARLY HALLSTATT	1100–1000	I	b	Rafaila, Jupalnic Predeal etc.	G	A_2	XI c.
EARLY HALLSTATT	1000–900	II	a	Moigrad, Teuteu, Brăduț, Sălard etc.	H	B_1	X c.
EARLY HALLSTATT	900–800	II	b	Fizeșul Gherlei, Hida, Gușterița etc.	I	B_2	IX c.
MIDDLE HALLSTATT	800–700	III	a	Firiteaz, Boarta, Bîia, Mihăileni etc.	J (Thraco-Cimmerian Horizon)	B_3	VIII c.
MIDDLE HALLSTATT	700–600	III	b	Bîrlad, Vînț, Bîlvănești etc.	L (Thraco-Cimmerian Horizon)	C	

Fig. 54. Tentative chronology and classification of the Iron Age hoards in Romania

sherds of ritually broken vessels. At Popești (near Bucharest) a stratum comprising two levels was identified; from the upper level a bronze fibula of the simple arched type with a triangular plate of the Blinckenberg III type (first half of the sixth century BC) was recovered.

Metal objects, mostly tools, weapons and ornaments, are made of bronze or iron. From the Popești site comes a flanged, *Fig. 55* flat iron axe which is an evolved variant and therefore later than the type from the Bîrlad hoard. Ornaments as well as weapons from the south-west area (Oltenia) are of Illyrian make (see the Basarabi cemetery). Also found were hand querns and small bone implements. The pottery can be divided into three types: a) coarse ware limited to only a few forms (bag-shaped or bell urns, very shallow bowls, some with decoration); b) an intermediate type more carefully worked than the first, usually of a darker fabric; and c) fine and very fine ware, of many shapes and types with decoration of a novel character. The last-named, which constitutes the third and last channelled-ware horizon, is mechanically burnished black ware with a metallic shine, decorated in the manner of pottery of the previous channelled-ware horizon but showing an improved technique. The most characteristic shapes include the following: biconical urns used by the Hallstatt people since the Pecica phase and of a form representing a new stage in the evolution of the Pecica culture; richly ornamented cups on a high pedestal; jugs with one

Fig. 55. a, Bronze fibula and socketed axe. Height of 1, 18cm., 2 to scale. b, Flanged iron flat-axe. Length, 26.8cm. From the Bîrlad board.

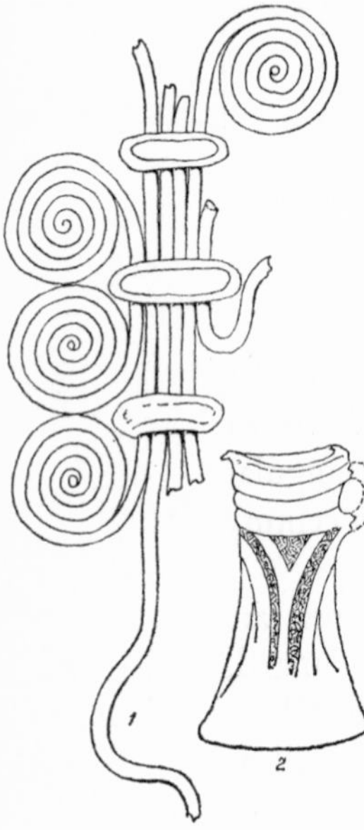

a

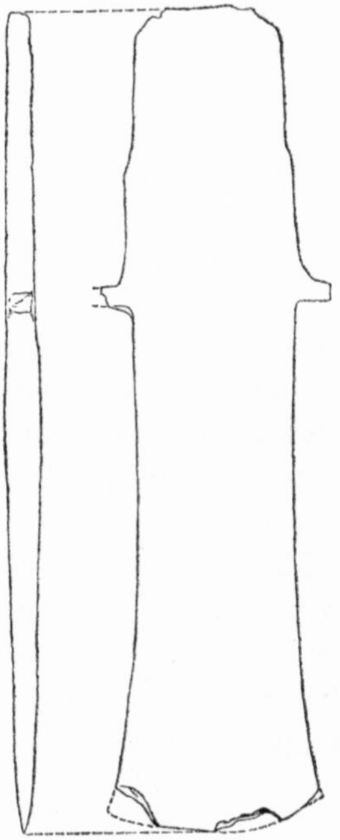

b

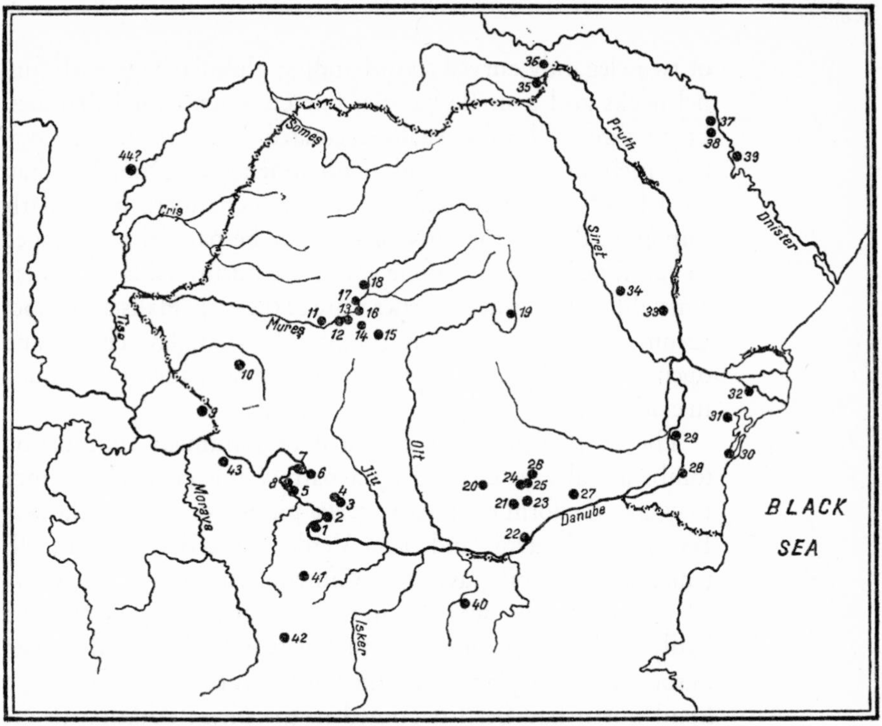

Fig. 56. Distribution of the Basarabi culture

1 Basarabi
2 Hunia
3 Verbicioara
4 Verbiţa
5 Balta Verde
6 Vînjuleţ
7 Ostrovul Corbului
8 Ostrovul Mare
9 Vattina
10 Vişagu
11 Rapoltu Mare
12 Tărtăria
13 Sibişeni
14 Răhău
15 Tilişca
16 Sebeş
17 Alba Iulia
18 Aiud
19 Bita
20 Blejeşti
21 Naipu
22 Giurgiu
23 Tangîru
24 Novaci
25 Popeşti
26 Bucharest
27 Curcani
28 Hîrşova
29 Cernavoda
30 Histria
31 Babadag
32 Murighiol
33 Bujor
34 Poiana
35 Herţa
36 Ţinteni
37 Alčedar
38 Şoldăneşti
39 Orşova
40 Devetaki
41 Dolni Lom
42 Vîlcitrîn
43 Židovar
44 Tószeg (?)

or two elegantly curved strap-handles; globular pots with funnel necks and a single handle; fine cups with small handles; broad-rimmed bowls usually decorated on the inside. Decoration includes applied bands with indentations, notches, hatched bands incrusted with white paste; channels, particularly important during the early phase, may be parallel or arranged in curvilinear designs. Some vessels are burnished to give them a metallic shine as in the better ware of the early Hallstatt period. *Fig. 57* Geometric motifs such as rhomboids, triangles, circles and open S-shaped spirals or continuous spiral patterns are much in evidence.

The dead were either cremated or inhumed. Inhumation tombs are always covered by a barrow but cremation tombs may take the form of either *pozzetto* pit-graves, such as those at Blejești in Muntenia and Balta Verde (Gura Blahniței) in Oltenia, or simple pit graves as at Ciurelu (Bucharest). The Gura Blahniței pit-grave was dug in the sand and then covered by a badly fired, chaff-tempered earthenware lid, which had broken as soon as it was placed over the tomb. At the time of burial, a hand quern had been deposited in the pit in addition to the typical pottery vessels described above. In spite of the complicated structure of the Basarabi culture, it is possible to trace the main lines of its evolution by means of the pottery; this derives its forms from those of the local early Hallstatt culture, which had itself inherited the rich material from the late and final Bronze Age. The biconical urn, however, marks a new stage of evolution during this period; whereas the high pedestalled cup, the origin of which goes back to the Vattina-Gîrla Mare culture, derives directly from a previous form found in the Vîrtop pottery. Also to be traced back to the final Bronze Age and the previous Hallstatt period is a type of large open bowl richly ornamented on the inside. Even the Vîlcitrîn handled lid can be found to have antecedents in the Carpatho-Danubian area. From the early Thracian Hallstatt on, the black burnished

Fig. 57. Large Basarabi-type dish from a shaft-grave at Blejești. Diameter, 49.5cm.

channelled ware with a metallic sheen is distributed throughout the same area. Incrusted and impressed ware had already been used during the second half of the Bronze Age. The typically Basarabi decorative motifs, such as the classical or the S-shaped spiral and other geometric designs (rhomboids, triangles, circles, etc.), developed locally. The Basarabi ware still retains elements from the Transylvanian Wietenberg and Noua cultures. Survivals of the Noua culture are also detectable in the Basarabi-type finds made at Alba Iulia ('Lumea Nouă', 1962), and at Sibișeni (in the Sibiu Museum). It would seem, therefore, that the Basarabi culture stemming from the local parent stock of the early Hallstatt horizon incorporates an important Thracian element including almost all the Carpatho-Danubian Bronze Age cultures, which had already become intermixed as a result of interpenetration during phase V. The period of the Basarabi horizon witnessed a veritable renascence of the spiral decoration.

The Basarabi culture came into being before the end of the Hallstatt IIb period, as the finds at 'Lumea Nouă' and other sites show. There is evidence of links with the early phase of the Thraco-Cimmerian horizon.

The Basarabi culture shows three main phases of development: (1) Basarabi I (about 800–750 BC), evidenced by the pit-graves at Blejești and Balta Verde (the flat cemetery at Gura Blahniței), the finds at Alba Iulia, the Vîlcitrîn treasure, etc. (in Italy this phase is assigned to the proto-Etruscan period); (2) Basarabi II (about 750–700 BC) characterized by the finds from Ciurelu, Poiana and Șoldănești; and (3) Basarabi III (about 700–650 BC) which is apparently limited geographically to southern Oltenia (the Basarabi cemetery where burial was by inhumation). Metal equipment shows a marked Illyrian influence. In their economic life the Basarabi people were chiefly occupied with stock-breeding, agriculture playing only a secondary role. A refined artistic sense is to be detected in some of their artifacts, for example, their decorated vessels, while the treasures such as that of Vîlcitrîn reflect a hierarchical society based on the accumulation of wealth. Bearers of this culture can be traced to the northern branch of the Thracian peoples.

The Balta Verde Group During the Hallstatt III period, certain more limited cultural groups also appeared on Romanian territory; these to a certain extent followed the lines of the Basarabi culture and did not, in general, break the pattern of local ethnic and cultural Thracian unity. One of these groups was the Balta Verde horizon of south-west Oltenia, which represents the Illyrian ethnic element also to be seen in Banat. Tumulus graves and several related sites provide the evidence. The barrows usually contain several tombs; by 1956, 27 funeral mounds had been excavated containing 67 tombs, 20 of which were those of warriors. The dead were placed, in an extended position, either on a bed of pebbles or directly on the bottom of a simple rectangular pit, which was then filled with earth or stones. Tomb 4 of tumulus XII contained the skeleton of a woman with rich grave goods, suggesting that, as with the Illyrians, women played an important role during the Iron Age. Two heavy bronze spectacle-fibulae, with an iron plaque and clasp, were placed on the chest, and there were two coiled spiral bracelets – one on each arm, – a torque of twisted bronze wire and, near the ears, four bronze-wire rings and a bronze hook.

Of the twenty warriors' tombs only one in tumulus II yielded remains of a chariot; from this same tomb were recovered the familiar pieces of harness decorated with filigree-work, and the side-pieces and bar of a bronze bit (*psalia*). The most important weapons were the leaf-shaped, lenticular-sectioned spear-heads from 20 to 41 cm. long. There was also the curved single-edged sabre-dagger with a cross-bar on the hilt giving it a T-shape; this is the typical Illyrian weapon widely distributed in the area of the Iron Gates, where influences from the Thracian world were felt. There are also the usual iron knives and sand-stone whetstones.

Among the personal ornaments, which are extremely numerous, were found bronze or iron fibulae and some made of a mixture of both metals; they are almost exclusively of the Glasinac type and have two springs with a rectangular or trapeze-shaped plate and an additional plate in the form of a 'Boeotian shield', bangles and ankle-rings made of bronze or iron (the body in tomb 2 of tumulus XVII wore four rings, two of bronze and two of iron on the right foot, and no less than nine iron rings on the left foot); also glass beads, buttons, applied ornaments, pendants, spirals, etc. Metal objects, as at Basarabi, show signs of a strong Illyrian influence; the pottery is virtually a local development linked to the previous Thracian elements and covering a large zone which takes in the finds made in north-west Bulgaria. The skeleton in tomb 2 of tumulus XVII, already referred to, bore on its chest a large stone block weighing 60 kg., whilst a boar's tusk had been plunged into the chest of another (no doubt to prevent the ghost from walking).

From the chronological point of view many of the finds in Oltenia and Banat, as well as in the neighbouring regions of Yugoslavia and Bulgaria, belong to the Balta Verde group, datable in general to the Hallstatt IIIb period (650–550 BC), after the first phase of the Basarabi culture and before the Gogoșu group. Studies of skeletons from the Balta Verde cemetery showed various anthropological types, and opinions are divided as to whether the people buried there and in corresponding cemeteries belonged ethnically to the Thracian or the Illyrian group.

The Stoicani Group At Stoicani, in south Moldavia, there is evidence of a Hallstatt horizon during which the dead were inhumed in a contracted position in graves not covered by mounds. This persistence of the old tradition is found also, among other places, in the Hallstatt cemetery at Valea Lupului, near Jassy. Fifty-five tombs have been excavated in Stoicani, many without grave goods and others with very poor equipment compared with that from Balta Verde; weapons are entirely lacking. The inhabitants were apparently concerned only with agriculture and stockbreeding with no interest in warlike activities, although historically the epoch was one of military democracy. Pottery predominated in the grave furniture, the vessels most commonly encountered being cups with a single
Fig. 58 strap-handle (there are fewer with two), bowls with everted rims and oblique and parallel channels decorating the carination. Some of the pots are large, like those of the Balta Verde group. Farther to the south-west of Romania another prevalent type is the vase on a high hollow pedestal with a channelled decorated neck and two small handles (*cf.* the Gruia assemblage in Oltenia). There is also a certain amount of coarse

Fig. 58. 1, Whetstone and 2–6, pottery from the Hallstatt cemetery at Stoicani (Moldavia). Length of 1, 5·7cm., pottery to scale

ware, such as beakers, biconical urns, etc. Both metal objects and tools of bone and stone are extremely rare. Only one tomb afforded a stone mace-head, though bronze ankle-rings are more frequent. In accordance with general practice in the Thraco-Illyrian world during Hallstatt times the tombs contained small, simple and slightly curved iron knives. Two Glasinac fibulae were also found in two children's tombs. This find, together with that from Șoldănești, marks the farthest point of distribution towards the north-east of this type of object. The excavator of this cemetery has identified two phases, of which the earlier covers the seventh century BC and the later developed during the sixth century BC. However, certain articles found in the tombs appear to be early, and could perhaps be attributed to the settlement situated on a hill-top known as 'Cetățuia', only 150 metres from the cemetery. At this settlement a Hallstatt II horizon has been detected as well as another pertaining to the early phase of Hallstatt III, and there are other Basarabi elements. At Stoicani there is the coeval settlement of

Tămăoani, containing also remains of a later date. Anthropological analysis of the bone material from Stoicani has revealed the presence of a predominantly Mediterranean type.

Gura Padinei The few widely-spread regional groups existing at this time do not break the general unity even though, in places, such as Gura Padinei, near Corabia (Oltenia) the dead are already being cremated and Thraco-Cimmerian elements also begin to appear.

Discoveries made during the past fifteen years have provided evidence in plenty that the phase III Hallstatt culture was in existence throughout Romanian territory, and that there was a continuity between it and the preceding period from which it derives. Chronologically, the Romanian Hallstatt III phase finished about 600–500 BC, before the Scythian influence was felt, and it may therefore be termed the 'pre-Scythian' period. Certain elements of this phase continued to develop during the late Hallstatt (IV), while others were diffused over a wider area, but it is impossible to distinguish any definite evolution; a case in point is the Frög ware from Carinthia, which has analogies with the Basarabi ware.

THE LATE PHASE OF THE LOCAL HALLSTATT

Locally there is no break in continuity between the Hallstatt III and the subsequent period. Similarly no interruption is noticeable in the gradually intensified relations between the regions situated on either side of the Carpathians or the Danube.

The fourth stage in the local Hallstatt begins about 600–550 BC, and finishes about 300 BC; these datings, however, do not apply to all of Romanian territory. In the Danubian-Pontic zone, the Hallstatt period was over by the middle of the fifth century BC; and it is only in the north Thracian zone that Hallstatt continues until about 300 BC. We must therefore differentiate between one region and another when considering

Plates 51, 54, 55

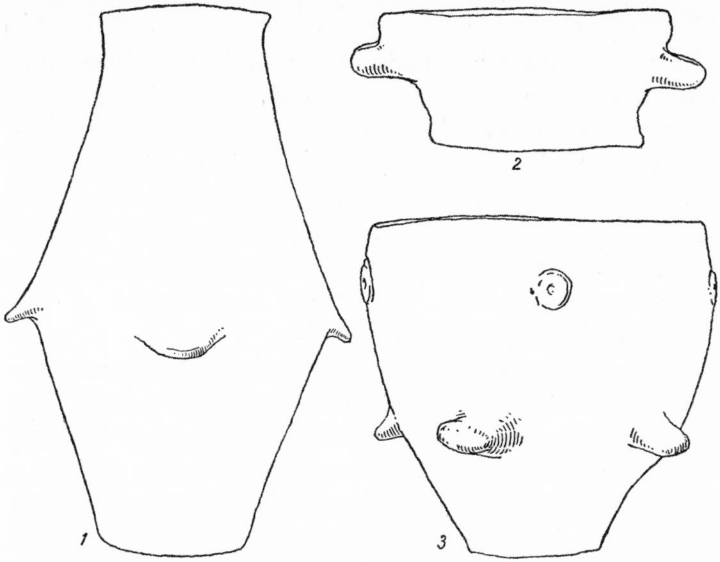

Fig. 59. Hallstatt pottery from Tariverde. Sixth century BC

the late Hallstatt in Romania as a whole. In evolutionary terms the Hallstatt IV stage can be seen to pass through three sub-phases.

Four main elements went to make up the late Hallstatt culture: 1) Local stock developed from the previous period; this is clearly evidenced in the pottery; the main styles of which – bowls, cups with one or two strap-handles, 'urns' of a biconical type, have evolved from previous forms. The same is also true of certain implements and personal ornaments. 2) The Greek component, originating on the west coast of the Black Sea, where centres of a more advanced civilization had been established during the seventh century BC. Evidence of this is provided by Hellenic imports obtained by means of barter between the local Thracian aristocracy and the Greek merchants. These point to an advanced stage of social and economic life having been reached by the local population, who were

Fig. 59

able to assimilate the goods of the Hellenic culture; they provide, furthermore, a means of dating the local cultures. Also to be considered are the local imitations of Greek models; these increase towards the end of the indigenous La Tène culture, and even faster thereafter. To be mentioned are the clay copies of the Greek *lebes* and the *oenochoi.* 3) The artifacts resulting from local and Greek forms interacting upon one another – as for example, vases with one or two strap-handles. 4) The Scythian or 'pseudo-Scythian' element.

THE BÎRSEŞTI-FERIGILE CULTURE
Fig. 61

During the late Hallstatt period a recently identified culture developed in the Sub-Carpathian region, later spreading towards the plain and into the Danube valley. Evidence is mainly confined to cemeteries of barrows. One of these occurs at Bîrsești, in the Focșani district, where 28 of the 40 tumuli in this cemetery were excavated between 1955 and 1958. These rather small tumulus graves contained single cremation burials. Frequently the same mound was used for secondary burials; near the burnt remains four or five vases had been placed, as well as other objects such as weapons (triple-ribbed arrowheads, iron double-bladed battle-axes, *akinakes*-type daggers), fibulae, glass beads, cruciform applied ornaments of zoomorphic type. Prevalent among the pottery shapes are bowls with everted rims, cups with a strap-handle, and bag-shaped pots. Two kinds of battle-axes are found, the Thracian type with two opposed blades and the Scythian type with a cutting edge at one end and a hammer-head at the other. Associated with them were bowls, made on a potter's wheel, of a grey fabric and similar in form to the hand-made examples. This cemetery dated to 550–450 BC, can be attributed to a Thracian group whose culture, developing from specifically local stock, already includes elements belonging to the Scythian culture, such as the four *akinakes* daggers, a weapon which the local population, like the Ferigile folk and the Razgrad people (from north Bulgaria), had already adapted. In fact the Bîrsești cemetery,

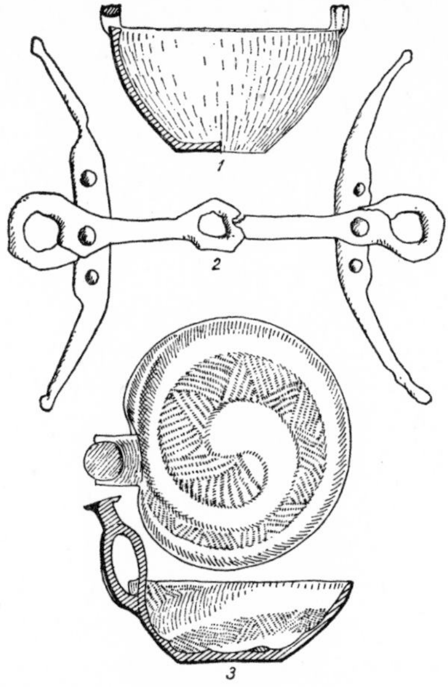

Fig. 60. Pottery and iron bridle-bit from the Ferigile cemetery (Oltenia)

similar sites in Moldavia and north Dobrudja, as well as the Ferigile cemetery in north Oltenia, in the Sub-Carpathian region, all form part of the same cultural horizon. The Ferigile cemetery comprises about 500 tumulus graves, many of a flat type, containing cremation burials. Ashes of the dead were placed in small pots or an urn and occasionally covered by a lid. Pottery, clearly deriving from that of the earlier horizon and *Fig. 60*

Fig. 61. Hand-worked (1) and turned 2) pottery from the tumulus cemetery at Bîrsești. Height of 1, 6.9cm., of 2, 12cm.

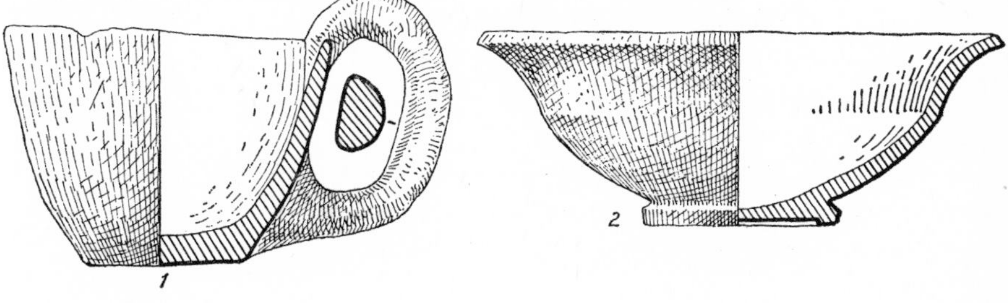

having affinities with the Bîrsești ware, includes the distinctive studded-vase with strap-handle. Decoration consists of excised spiral decoration, channels and grooves. The frequent use of the channel decoration and the spiral motif relates the Ferigile to the Basarabi culture; recently (1963) I myself identified this archaizing aspect at the rich site of Govora-sat, near Rîmnicu-Vîlcea. At Ferigile there are also several *akinakes* daggers (as at Bîrsești), Thracian double-axes (of the Bîlvănești type), Scythian hammer-axes, flanged-iron axes, applied ornaments like those from Balta Verde, horse-bits, Glasinac-type fibulae, etc. The Ferigile cemetery is datable to the sixth-seventh centuries BC and attests the existence of a Thracian assemblage in the Sub-Carpathian region.

Fig. 60

THE GOGOȘU GROUP

Meanwhile, in the Danube valley and in south-west Oltenia, a new group – though it maintained contacts with the Bîrsești-Ferigile – developed from the Balta Verde culture.

Archaeological evidence for this is provided by the tumulus cemetery at Gogoșu, near Balta Verde, where more than 70 barrows were discovered, about 50 of which contained earlier interments, the rest being later cremation burials. The eleven warrior's tombs contained spearheads, double axes, fibulae both of a Glasinac-type and a Donja-Dolina type (with a triangular plate at one end), two fibulae of the *navicella* type, an Illyrian pin, bangles, glass beads, and among other pottery a single-handled wheel-made pot datable to the fifth century BC. The cemetery is a fifth-century one, though some of the tombs may date from the fourth century. As in the Gruia finds, a certain Illyrian influence is detectable in the Gogoșu culture. Other sites also in or on the borders of the Carpathian region of Romania have afforded artifacts similar to those of the cultures discussed above.

THE SCYTHIANS

Until some three decades ago it was believed that the Scythians had made violent incursions westwards and been a dominant factor for several centuries. Since then, however, it has become more generally accepted that there was in fact a greater ethnic and cultural continuity where the local population was concerned. Archaeological evidence is now more plentiful, and field reports have thrown new light on the problem of the Thraco-Scythian relationship within the Carpatho-Danubian zone. Specific studies and monographs based on archaeological findings have thrown much light on the historical context within which the Scythian problem should be considered. The Scythians as well as the Greeks are known to have exerted influence in the area of the Lower Danube and the Carpathians, and both these elements affected the development of the indigenous population. Scythian influence did not, however, have such profound consequences in the Carpatho-Danubian region as did Greek influence in the Danubian-Pontic zone, even though the former was spread over a wider area. The earliest evidence of specifically Scythian elements on Romanian territory goes back no further than the middle of the sixth and the beginning of the fifth century BC. Characteristically Scythian are the ritual bronze cauldrons, one of which, hemispherical in shape, was found before the First World War in a mound at Scorțaru in the Muntenian Plain, the other at Castelu in Dobrudja in 1960; the latter, shaped like a portion of a sphere, is decorated with zig-zag designs in relief, and its handles are formed by two stylized wild goats. Both cauldrons date from the end of the fifth century BC. On the other hand, two bone *psalia*, incorporating primitive realistic animal designs, found at Histria and Tariverde in a cultural level which the presence of archaic Greek pottery enables us to date to the second half of the sixth century BC, indicate an earlier Scythian influence in the Lower Danube. Similar evidence is provided by the iron handle of a mirror, taking the form of a stylized vulture, recovered from a Thracian tumulus grave in the cemetery at Histria, in a level corresponding to that in which the *psalia* was found; it falls within the period of the earliest series of

Fig. 62

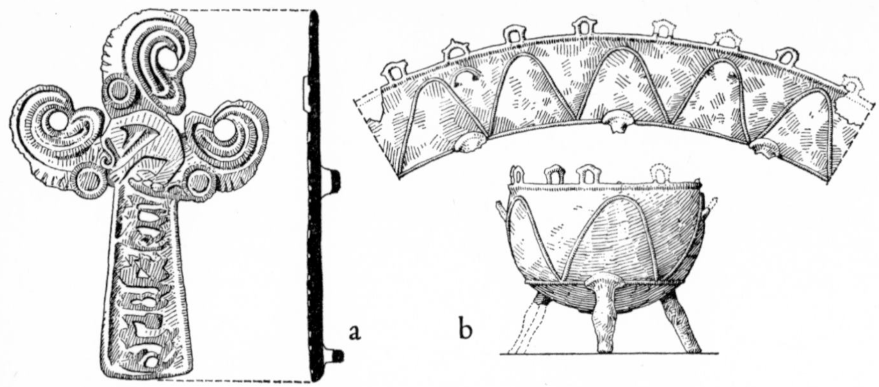

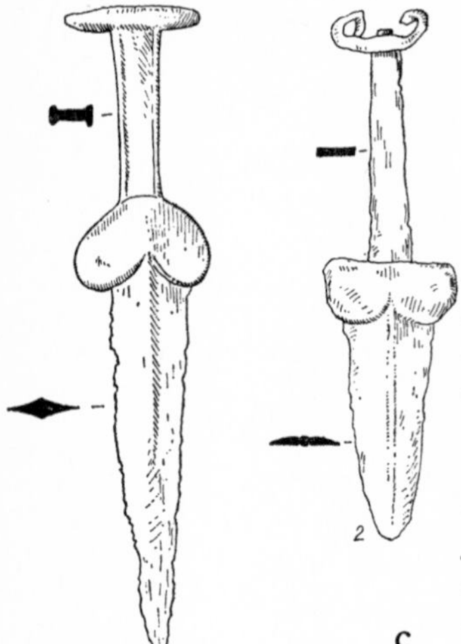

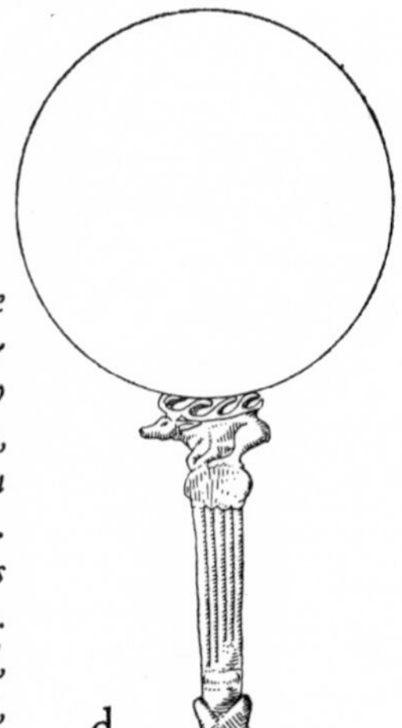

Fig. 62. a, Cruciform animal-style applied bronze ornament from a tumulus grave of the Hallstatt group at Bîrsești (after B. Mitrea). Height, 10.4cm. b, Scythian cauldron from Scorțaru (after V. Pîrvan, Getica*). Height, 65cm. c, Scythian daggers from Macișeni (1) and Cipău (2). Length of 1, 28cm, of 2, 19.5cm. d, Bronze mirror from Feiurd. Height, 72.6cm.*

'Scythian' or 'Thraco-Scythian' stone statues from the north Pontic steppes and Dobrudja (see the example from Stupina, datable to the middle of the fifth century BC and that from Sibiora). In addition, archaeological excavations at Histria and other sites in Dobrudja have revealed Hallstatt pottery that differs essentially from the Thracian ware: blackish or grey vases made of a fabric tempered with sand, potsherds and grit. The most characteristic vessel shape is the high-pedestalled goblet with an incurving rim pitted with small perforations; where the neck joins the body of the vase there is a raised band with round impressions. Vessels bearing the closest resemblance to this form are found north of the Black Sea. Thus, within the context of the eastern Hallstatt, a zone north-west of the Black Sea has been defined which reflects both local Thracian elements and the Scythian factor, as well as Greek influence. This group, which continued throughout the sixth century BC, originated in the last decade of the seventh. The archaizing aspect of Transylvanian 'Scythoid' or Scythian antiquities is explained by the 'Scythian' cultural element which, stemming from the forest lands of the steppes, exerted its influence from the first half of the sixth century onwards.

SOUTH THRACE AND THE CARPATHIANS

If the two ritual cauldrons – used for ceremonial rites which cannot easily be transmitted from one population to another – attest the presence, however temporary or sporadic, of the Scythians, links between the Scythians and the Thracians are more positively indicated by the other evidence mentioned above. There was, in fact, contact between the Thraco-Getian zone of the southern Thracians and that of the Scythians in the north Pontic steppes, where the 'Royal Scythians', described by Herodotus, exercised their dominating and supreme authority. The relationship between the Scythians and the northern Thracians from the Carpathian zone presents an entirely different problem. While in the Danubian-Pontic zone Scythian influence was spreading at a time when the transition to the La Tène was already beginning, in the Carpathian region the Scythian or pseudo-Scythian element came into contact with an unaltered Hallstatt culture. The presence of Scythian, or rather, 'Scythoid' elements (a number of *akinakes* daggers from Transylvania and north Moldavia, mirrors with zoomorphic handles, cruciform or zoomorphic applied ornaments, and even certain forms of ritual adopted by the indigenous inhabitants, etc.) in the areas inhabited by the north Thracians can be ex- *Fig. 62* plained by the close and prolonged relationship of the Thracians of the north with the 'Scythians' and the rest of the heterogeneous peoples living in the wooded steppes, in whom the Thracian element was unlikely to be absent. There is now evidence to show that even the *akinakes*, for long regarded as the Scythian 'national' weapon, had also been adopted by the Thracians; indeed, excavations at Ferigile and Bîrsești have revealed *akinakes* actually in the tombs of Thracian warriors. The *akinakes* from Razgrad, in north Bulgaria can be explained in this light. The Thracian cemetery at Bîrsești also yielded a cruciform applied ornament of zoomorphic type, showing clear Greek influence. The purely Scythian component of the finds from ostensibly Scyth-influenced Transylvania, from the Kustanovice group, or from the 'Scythian' Hallstatt of Slovakia and Hungary, is extremely small compared with that encountered in the Danubian-Pontic zone. Even the *akinakai* from Transylvania, the Sub-Carpathian zone and Hungary assume forms representing variants associated with areas peripheral to the strictly Scythian ethnic area. The sword from Dobolii de Jos associates central European Hallstatt features with the Scythian zoomorphic style, while the type of sword found in Penc in Hungary also occurs in the western region of the east Carpathians. Finally, an analysis of bones from the culture recently discovered at Ciumbrud has revealed a high proportion of brachycephalic elements, which would decisively rule out the anthropological type that distinguishes the Scythians of U.S.S.R. territory. As regards the actual presence of Iranian-speaking Scythians on Romanian territory, we can at present do no more than postulate temporary incursions by groups of warriors. It was not until the beginning of the second half of the fourth century BC that the Scythians tried a violent and massive penetration into territory inhabited by the Thraco-Getians. This was at the time of Atheas, the *rex Istrianorum*, chief of the Thraco-Getian tribal union in the Lower Danube, as well as of

Fig. 63

Fig. 63. 'Scythian' sword from Dobolii-de-Jos. Length, 1.135m.

King Philip II of Macedon. The Scythians met Getian resistance and had later to face Macedonian methods in these parts. There are only sporadic signs of the presence of Scythians to the south of the Danube in what was to become *Scythia Minor* during the third century BC, and they did not play the important role that pre-war historians attributed to them.

Nevertheless, contacts with the Scythian world contributed – particularly during the final Hallstatt and the initial phase of La Tène – to the wider diffusion of iron metallurgy and to the distribution of cultural equipment of eastern origin (zoomorphic designs and some elements of the distant Greek civilization) to areas beyond south-east Europe. The Scythian or 'Scythoid' legacy persists in the La Tène Getian and Geto-Dacian culture. The Scythians from the steppes also made their contribution towards the birth of Thracian art and of the Thraco-Scythian style in the Lower Danube.

CHAPTER VIII

The Second Iron Age: La Tène

THE TRANSITION TO THE SECOND IRON AGE

INTERNAL FACTORS caused the Thracian Hallstatt culture to develop at different rate in different areas. After establishing sporadic contacts with the inhabitants of these regions, Greek merchants received, during the last decades of the seventh century BC, constant and valuable support from among the ranks of the local, and particularly the higher, aristocracy in the Milesian colony of Histria which had become a centre for the diffusion of the Hellenic civilization. Excavations at Histria have provided important archaeological evidence concerning the material culture of the seventh and subsequent centuries; this strongly reflects the Thracian element, which is to be seen even in the Greek dwellings of the colony and in the cemetery there, as well as in the cemeteries at Tariverde, Vadu and elsewhere. Primitively hand-worked pottery was gradually replaced by wheel-made ware. The development of crafts and increase of barter led to the appearance of exchange

Fig. 64

tokens; this 'money' takes the form of triple-ribbed arrowheads (known as the 'Scythian' type), examples of which have been found at the site of Tariverde and in hoards. The economy was still of a mixed type, with agriculture and stock-breeding as its two main supports. At the time when the Greeks settled in Histria, the indigenous population, being culturally advanced with a high standard of living, the Thraco-Getian aristocracy were in a position to assimilate the elements of the Hellenic civilization. This aristocracy actively encouraged contacts and trade with the Greeks. The Greek element, by prompting local forces, contributed to the disintegration of community relationships and accentuated the uneven development of

Fig. 64 'Scythian' arrowheads employed as currency from Jurilovca (1–3) and Tariverde (4, 5). Length of 1, 4.8cm., others to scale

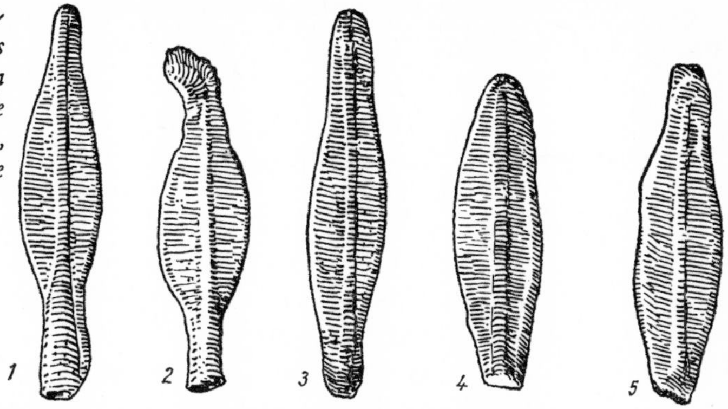

the Thracian world in general. The culture of the Hallstatt IV period, although remaining essentially Thracian in character, showed definite Hellenistic trends. This, however, applied only to members of the aristocracy. Certain forms of Greek ware, such as the *oenochoe*, the *lebes*, the pedestalled bowl with an incurving rim, the cup, etc., were imitated by local people; other forms, resulting from Greek imports, were absorbed into the equipment of the local culture which acquired the label 'aristocratic', as in west and central Europe. On the Black Sea coast and, to a lesser extent, in the entire Danubian-Pontic zone, the Greek element helped the local Thraco-Getians in their cultural development, while the communities in the north Thracian zone kept within the framework of a strictly Hallstatt way of life in spite of the penetration of several imported elements of Greek civilization.

The discoveries made during the last few years enable us to trace the rise of, and identify, the different stages in the La Tène civilization. In the region of the Lower Danube, the changes leading to the La Tène period go back to quite an early date, when the very structure of the late Hallstatt culture, already south Thracian in aspect, begins to be affected. Before long, economic and social differences became even more ac- *Fig. 65* centuated. More and more local products (cereals, cattle, fish, honey and slaves, which are mentioned by Menander), were exchanged for Greek merchandise (oils, wines, precious materials, jewellery, fine quality pottery, such as that from Barboși, Galați, Frumușița, etc.); all with a view to satisfying the ever-increasing demands of the Thraco-Getian aristocracy which, from the sixth century onwards, enjoyed a life of luxury. For them, this century marks a new stage in their social, economic and cultural progress, owing to a great extent to the spread of Greek and Macedonian money.

The question of the origin of the La Tène culture in the Lower Danube arose when in 1954 a flat level cemetery of cremation burials containing covered urns surrounded by stones

Plate 53

was uncovered at Cernavoda. The grave furniture of the four tombs that were excavated showed three distinct influences: firstly, the purely local Thracian Hallstatt; secondly, the La

Plates 51, 54, 55

Tène in its initial stages; and lastly, the Hellenistic. The last-named element is represented by an imported luxury article, a bronze mirror with an iron handle, found in the funerary urn of a local woman aristocrat. Four main pottery shapes belonging to the Thracian Hallstatt have been identified: the bell-pot, the bag-pot, the biconical urn and the bowl with an incurving rim, representing the traditional local stock unaffected by foreign influences. However, the slim biconical vase with a strap-handle and the hemispherical pedestalled bowl without a handle but of a finer fabric reflect on the one hand the first influences of Greek civilization in the Danube valley (on the coast these were manifested earlier), on the other hand the beginning of the gradual change to La Tène. Vessels with a single handle, such as that from Cernavoda were found also at Frumușița in south Moldavia, associated with a *kylix* of Attic provenance and datable to the first half of the fifth century BC; similar finds were made in Muntenia and Oltenia. Hand-made vessels with a single strap-handle mark the beginning of La

Chronology: Relative	Chronology: Date	Phases	Reinecke	Tischler-Dechelette	V. Pîrvan
EARLIEST LA TÈNE	500 (450) – 400	I	A	I	Geto-Scythian Iron Age
EARLY LA TÈNE	400 – 300	II	B		
MIDDLE LA TÈNE	300 – 200 – 100 B.C.	III a, b	C 1, 2	II	II
LATE LA TÈNE	100 B.C. – 106 A.D.	IV a, b	D	III	III 1, 2
FINAL LA TÈNE	106 A.D. – 200 – 300 (271)	V a, b			
PERIOD OF MIGRATIONS					

Fig. 65. Tentative chronology of the Late Iron Age (La Tène) in Romania

Tène in the Danubian-Pontic zone. This is a type that evolved from the traditional local Thracian forms and developed during the Geto-Dacian La Tène period simultaneously with the wheel-made ware. The latter derived from Greek prototypes arriving through Thraco-Getian channels.

LA TÈNE I: 450–400 BC

Finds made on the left bank of the Danube, at Alexandria, Chirnogi, and elsewhere indicate that, as a result of the Greek cultural influx, the potter's wheel was already used in some places by the local inhabitants at the end of the sixth century BC: its use during the following century is unquestionable. Perhaps at this period the Thraco-Getians of the Danubian region already had improved agricultural implements, but for the moment no precise archaeological evidence of this is available. Evidence from Frumușița, București-Tei and Coțofeni suggests that Greek imports, particularly painted ware, penetrated deeper into the lands inhabited by the Thraco-Getians. In the west zone of Romania products of Greek influence spread from the time of the Illyrians onwards; such objects, for example, as the silver hinged fibulae from the Ostrovul Mare treasure, and the Greco-Illyrian-type helmet from Gostavăț on the right bank of the Olt, both in Oltenia. A tomb excavated at Ostrovul Mare yielded an Illyrian-type pin associated with a hand-made *oenochoe* of fine grey ware. During the same La Tène I phase the Greek *lebes* was also imitated but it was distributed by way of the southern Thracians. During the fourth and third centuries BC this type of vase spread from the Danubian-Pontic zone to the mountainous region of the Carpathians – the Bîrsești-Ferigile assemblage is a case in point – and was later incorporated into the archaeological equipment of La Tène. The earliest La Tène or Proto-La Tène horizon begins, as already mentioned, earlier on the Black Sea coast than in the inland territories inhabited by the Geto-Dacians. The finds at Alexandria, which include rich wheel-made pottery, are also apparently early in type; and in this cultural context the Glasinac fibula persists. Other sites in the zone extending from the Iron Gates to south Moldavia, and inland as far as the Carpathians, have afforded wheel-made pottery of south Thracian origin. Chronologically the Proto-La Tène horizon begins about the middle of the fifth century BC, and it is at this time that the Thraco-Getian La Tène culture first appears. At the outset the Greek element played the most important role, to be joined later by the Scythian element from the steppes north of the Black Sea. Even after the Thraco-Getian La Tène culture had been firmly established, the South Thracian element – in its strictest and most limited sense – continued to influence the Danubian-Pontic zone, and through this the Dacian zone proper.

LA TÈNE II: 400–300 BC

Throughout the fourth century the life led by the Thraco-Getians from the Danube and the Pontic zone was, on both the material and spiritual plane, wholly La Tène in character; at the same time it had progressed in every sphere. The century, in fact, marks the final floruit of the Thraco-Getian civilization in the Lower Danube. In both the settlements and the cemetery the continuity between the Hallstatt and the LaTène periods is attested throughout the Danubian-Pontic zone and in east and north-east Bulgaria. The potter's wheel is in use everywhere, and the work of the potter becomes a specialized craft. At the same time Greek coins minted in the Pontic colonies are more widely distributed. The dead were mostly cremated and the ashes placed in lidded urns. A cemetery of flat tombs was excavated at Murighiol and another with cremation tombs under tumuli at Teliţa, both in Dobrudja. It was in the latter that a large mound containing seven tombs was discovered, the most important of which contained rich grave goods no doubt belonging to an eminent member of the local aristocracy. North of the Danube, interesting fourth-century finds were made at the Getian settlement and tumulus cemetery of Zimnicea. The first horizon of this culture, the development of which can be followed right through to the end of the second century, belongs in fact to the fourth century BC. One tomb discovered here deserves special mention; it was constructed with undressed river boulders and the grave goods consisted of weapons (iron spearheads, a Chalcidian-type bronze helmet), an iron fibula, several imported amphorae and other objects. At Zimnicea there were also several wheel-turned vessels, resembling in shape and fabric those found throughout the world of the south Thracians. At Zimnicea a wheel-made vase with a stamped rosette decoration was found; a further example of this type of vase is found in the material from Ocnița, in Oltenia. Another Getian settlement site of the La Tène period, identified at Piroboridava (Ptolemy, *Geogr.* IV, 10,8), is at Poiana on the left bank of the Siret, in Moldavia.

The first local coinage apparently came into circulation in the Thraco-Getian world also during the fourth century. As recently as 1964 a new type of Getian coin was discovered in Dobrudja which bore the inscription BASILEOS MOSKONOS; nom. Moskon, in Greek letters. This was perhaps the name of a chief of one of the tribal unions that had come into being at the end of the fourth or beginning of the third century BC (rex Istrianorum?).

THRACIAN ART

A remarkable feature deserving very special attention is the growth, during the first two phases of the Thraco-Getian La Tène period, of Thracian art; by virtue of its excellent quality and its originality it compares favourable with Scythian art. It was the publication in 1959 of the blade-emblem from Medgidia that gave us the opportunity of revising earlier ideas

concerning Thracian and Scythian art; the question of the so-called 'Craiova treasure' was also reconsidered at this stage. Plate 58
The *akinakes*-shaped emblem-ornament form Medgidia, dating Plate 59
from the second half or the end of the fifth century BC, has no equal in all south-east Europe and the zone of Thracian and Plates 62-64
Scythian expansion. It was cast in bronze and was attached either to a commemorative funerary monument or to a normal tomb. The decoration makes use of characteristic Thracian and Scythian motifs, namely, a panther's head, a deer's neck and head with very stylized antlers, an equally stylized eagle's head with a serpent held in its beak. The last-named motif is representative of an early tradition found in the local Hallstatt art of the Balkans and the Danube; it was later to be widely used by the Geto-Dacians in their silver-work. Thus the technique and decorative motifs of the Romanian 'emblem' reveal elements common to all Thracian art, as exemplified by the 'Craiova treasure', the grave furniture from the Agighiol tomb, and that from Brădești (grasshopper-shaped ornaments), and by other material discovered in Bulgaria (Garčinovo, Radiuvene, Lukovit, Vraca, etc.). Nevertheless this article also incorporates a Scythian element, similar to that seen in the Melgunov-Kelermes-Sumejko and Vettersfelde series and other more recent finds. Hellenic influence is also discernible. The Thracian zoomorphic style, formed at the end of the fifth and the beginning of the fourth century BC, was the result of traditional Thracian trends having intermingled with naturalistic Scythian art; such a creative combination was favoured by the Hellenistic element common to both. Thracian art is a 'princely' art, like that of the Scythians from the north Pontic steppes.

The Agighiol 'Prince's' Grave One of the most important discoveries relating to the civilization and art of the Thraco-Getians in Romania is the grave at Agighiol, excavated in 1931 by I. Andrieșescu, aided by myself. It is a very large tumulus grave, situated on the hill of Babadag, near Agighiol, in north Dobrudja. The interior of the tumulus was constructed of dressed stone, and on some of the blocks Greek letter are engraved. There were two compartments: the main sepulchral chamber containing the skeleton of a man, and a small adjoining room containing that of a woman. Not far from this structure was a walled enclosure of undressed stones, built to serve as a tomb for three horses with all their harness, which was decorated with bronze and silver zoomorphic ornaments. A passage (*dromos*), filled with large stones after the funeral ceremony, leads to the main chamber. Near the male skeleton a large number of objects had been placed, among them triple-ribbed arrowheads (incorrectly referred to as of the 'Scythian' type), iron spearheads, a silver ceremonial helmet which had been partly gilded and which in technique and style resembled Plate 56 the helmet from Coțofănești, and two silver greaves decorated with raised gold ornaments combining zoomorphic and an- Plates 60, 61 thropomorphic designs. Two beautiful silver drinking-vessels (*hanaps*) were also found, decorated with scenes featuring fantastic animals, several silver pateras – one engraved, in Greek letters, with the name of *KOTYS*, probably the name of the deceased or that of the Thracian artisan (the same name also occurs in Vraca, Bulgaria). In various parts of this sepulchral chamber were found amphorae and other Greek vessels as well as sherds of red-figure Attic pottery of the fifth century BC. Near the female skeleton in the smaller chamber were gold-leaf earrings the shape of which is reproduced in the decoration of the greaves, and other articles of jewellery. Much of the grave furniture had clearly been stolen or partially destroyed by tomb-robbers at various times. The vase, which was first recorded as having originated in the 'Iron Gates region' and was published in 1936 by V. Griessmaier, by the author in 1941 and later by Jacobstahl, must actually have come from this same grave of Agighiol, seeing that it so strikingly resembles the one we reproduce.

Scythian influence is clearly discernible in the Agighiol tomb, both in the design of the works of art and in the ritual entailing the sacrifice of the wife and horses at the funeral ceremony. This find belongs to the category of Thraco-Getian 'aristocratic' or 'princely' monuments, the deceased having no doubt been one of the heads of the local aristocracy at the end of the fifth or beginning of the fourth century BC (that is to say, around 400).

The 'Prince's' Tomb of Craiova The so-called 'treasure of Craiova' falls into this same category of monuments. It was published under that name by H. Schmidt but in fact represents the grave furniture of another Thraco-Getian 'prince's' tomb, from elsewhere in the plains of Oltenia. Included are the 80 articles that it has been possible to retrieve. These comprise a variety of silver and sometimes gilded plaques used for ornamenting horse-harness: triangular or rectangular pieces, elongated plaques, applied ornaments shaped like a bull's head and sometimes gilded, and others representing two lions on a background of Thracian-type hatched bands, a frontal ornament in the form of a panther's head, and many more. Ornamental plaques of this kind constitute a specific feature of the Thraco-Getian civilization of the La Tène II period (or more precisely the second half of the third century BC), and reveal the unity, originality and individuality of the Thracians, as do the other finds described in these pages. Plate 58

The Gold Helmet from Coțofănești In 1929 at Coțofănești, near Poiana-Vărbilău (Muntenia), a gold helmet was discovered quite by chance. It proved to be a completely isolated find, though as a result of research undertaken at the site by I. Andrieșescu, the existence of an associated cultural horizon was revealed in the form of grey wheel-made ware showing Thracian and Geto-Thracian traits. The helmet is conical in shape with a rectangular facial opening. Above this opening are representations of two large eyes which were probably thought to Plate 57 possess supernatural powers. The cheek and neck guards are decorated with figures of fantastic animals, scenes showing sacrificial ceremonies, or spirals and other geometric designs. The rosette encountered both on the bull's heads in the 'Craiova treasure' and on the Thracian turned pots is here the dominant motif. This was almost certainly a ceremonial helmet belonging to an eminent member of the local aristocracy and can be dated to the same period as the finds at Agighiol; it was in fact at this time that a pronounced social hierarchy was being established among the Thraco-Getian aristocracy. The 'Craiova treasure' and the contemporary treasure containing gold objects discovered in 1960 at Băiceni near Cucuteni point to similar social distinctions; the latter included harness plaques with zoomorphic figures, the remains of a helmet, a bracelet, among other articles.

Rex Istrianorum The extent and efficiency of the Getian organization, within the framework of military democracy, became fully apparent from the second half of the fourth century BC onwards when the Scythians, under the leadership of Atheas, tried to force their way south of the Danube (Justin-Trogus IX, 2–3). Macedon, which had replaced the Odryses in this area, likewise intervened. The Scythians were thus not able to settle south of the Danube until the third and second centuries BC when they founded small political units in the zone between Callatis and Odessos. It was in the third century BC that the Dobrudja region acquired the name Scythia Minor.

LA TÈNE III: 300(280) – 100(75) BC

The beginning of the third century saw the establishment, in the Danubian-Pontic zone (in its widest geographical and cultural sense) and the Balkan-Danubian area, of a Thraco-Getian civilization of a fully developed La Tène type, which grew increasingly prosperous. It was advancing towards an oppidum life, almost urban in character, a phenomenon also attested by literary sources for areas north of the Danube (see Ptolemy's account in Strabo and Arrian). These texts also mention Alexander the Great's expedition beyond the Danube in 335 BC and that of General Zopyrion, the Governor of Thrace, in 326 BC. In 313 the Getians from Dobrudja were the allies of Callatis in his struggle against Lysimachos. By about 300, the Getians of Dobrudja and the Lower Danube had combined to form what was virtually a state, an evolved type of military democracy having as its leader the *basileus* Dromichaïtes, the conqueror of Lysimachos whose own state was based on an economic and social organization far superior to that of the Getians. The fourth century BC passed into the third with no discernible break in the material development of the Thraco-Getian La Tène culture. The standard of economic and cultural life rose, as shown by the large-scale distribution, in local centres, of Greek goods as well as coins from Macedonia and the Pontic towns. The discoveries made at such sites as Tariverde, Vadu, Murighiol, Satu Nou and Zimnicea, as well as other occasional finds, show that life in general continued to follow the La Tène pattern. Bands of Celtic warriors were not to reach western Romania, much less the Lower Danube, until after 300 BC. Greek cities on the west coast of the Black Sea found protectors and valuable allies in the Getian *basilei,* such as Zalmodegikos (whose name was revealed by an inscription found in 1959 at Histria) in the third century, Rhemaxos about 200 BC, and many others.

During the La Tène III period, this social and economic development of the local peoples of the Danubian-Pontic area went hand in hand with that of other Thracians south of the Danube and outstripped that of the people in the Carpathian zone. It should be stressed, therefore, that – until the events in the Lower Danube involving the struggle of Dromichaïtes and Lysimachos, when the routes of the Celts towards Rome were closed following the defeat of the Senones – it was only in the Danubian-Pontic zone that people had already attained the La Tène level of civilization, without the Celts having participated in the formation of this culture. When the Celts appeared in the Carpatho-Danubian region there was, therefore, a Thraco-Getian La Tène area, and another zone in the Carpathians where a purely Hallstatt cultural context prevailed. Such were the special circumstances in which the La Tène III period opened about 300 BC. It saw the culture of the Geto-Dacians reach a new stage in its development. Before long it extended over the entire territory inhabited by them, bringing with it new and improved equipment.

Fig. 66

LA TÈNE IV: 100 BC–AD 106

The period during which the father of King Burébista was leader of the Daco-Getians and taking in also the early part of the latter's reign corresponds to the transition phase to La Tène IV. This period occupied the first century BC (subphase IVa) and the first century AD (IVb) up to the time when Dacia was conquered by the Romans and the Dacian state was destroyed.

LA TÈNE V: AD 106 (15, DOBRUDJA)–300 (271)

Roman influence increased steadily during these two centuries. In the Pontic zone and along the Danube valley this influence was encountered even earlier. The Getians of Scythia Minor had already entered a new phase in their history after the Roman conquest of this region. In the other territories, the free Dacians developed their own traditional La Tène culture, although they were also subject to a strong and permanent Roman economic and cultural influence. Evidence of Dacian culture at this stage in its development has been discovered in Moldavia, north-west and west Romania, east Hungary,

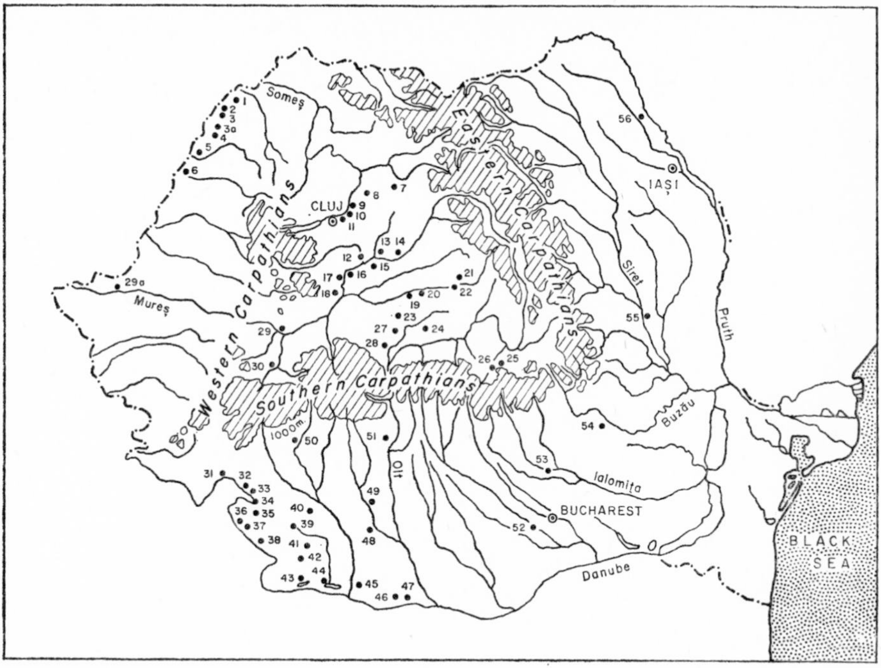

Fig. 66. The Celts in Romania

1 Ciumești
2 Curtuiușeni
3 Valea lui Mihai
3a Otomani
4 Săcuieni
5 Diosig
6 Sîntion
7 Galații Bistriței
8 Sîntioana
9 Jucul de Sus
10 Apahida
11 Dezmir
12 Luncani
13 Bandul de Cîmpie
14 Morești
15 Heria
16 Silivaș
17 Aiud
18 Craiva
19 Mediaș
20 Dupușul
21 Cristurul Săcuesc
22 Sedriaș
23 Vorumloc
24 Toarcla
25 Brașov
26 Rîșnov
27 Vurpăr
28 Sibiu
29 Ursin-Simeria
29a Pecica
30 Hațeg
31 Orșova
32 Turnu-Severin
33 Ostrovul Șimian
34 Ostrovul Corbului
35 Viașu
36 Balta Verde
37 Gruia
38 Gîrla Mică
39 Orodel
40 Gogoșița
41 Vîrtop
42 Corlatele
43 Rast
44 Plosca
45 Călărași
46 Gura Padinei
47 Orlea
48 Dobrosloveni
49 Băbeni
50 Cornești
51 Govora
52 Popești
53 Tinosu
50 Sărata Monteoru
55 Poiana
56 Glăvăneștii Vechi

Slovakia (see the Dacian culture of Puchovo), in the sub-Carpathian region of the Ukrainian S.S.R. and in the Moldavian S.S.R. (the Lipitza culture).

THE ROLE OF THE CELTS

Thirty years ago it was maintained that the Celts played a determining and unilateral role, affecting all the territories inhabitated by the Geto-Dacian people in a like manner; according to this theory it was the Celts who caused the local inhabitants to advance into the Second Iron Age.

In the Carpatho-Danubian region the Celts found an historical and cultural milieu entirely different from that which they had encountered in central Europe, north Italy, Great Britain and the Balkans. It is only necessary to mention two factors to illustrate the point: 1) When they came to the Carpathians, which they sought to cross in order to reach the mouths of the Danube and the Greek towns near the Black Sea, the Celts found a local La Tène culture already established as well as a military and political organization under the *basileus* Dromichaïtes mentioned in the Greek texts. 2) As they had already done to some extent in Slovakia and Hungary, the Celts encountered in Romania Scythian or pseudo-Scythian elements mixed with hardy local parent stock.

The earliest finds attributable to the time when the first group of Celtic warriors made incursions east of the Tisa, on Romanian territory, do not date back further than 300–280 BC. Consequently the first influence of the Celtic element in the Carpathians and on the Danube were felt at the beginning of the La Tène III period, that is, during the second great phase of Celtic expansion. Two factors may be taken into account for the presence of Celts on Romanian territory at that particular time. On the one hand there was the barrier presented by Rome after the defeat of the Senones, which led to the regrouping of the Celts massed in the north-west Balkans. On the other hand there was the disorganization of Macedonian and Thracian military and state power, and this facilitated the incursion of Celtic warriors into almost all parts of the Balkans. It appears that the wave of Celtic invasions, which was broken at Delphi in the winter of 279–278 BC, reached certain areas of south-west Romania, in particular Oltenia. Spreading from the west, and deployed over a wide front between the Mureş and Someş rivers, the armed groups of Celts also advanced towards Transylvania. They penetrated the rich lands of this province by way of the Mureş, Tîrnave and Someş valleys and then along those of the Crişuri and the Bereteu. Supplementing the archaeological finds from Transylvania are those from Moldavia, east of the Carpathians, but these are best considered in relation to the Celtic penetration from north of the range, close to the south-west U.S.S.R. in the direction of the Crimea. South of the Carpathians, contact with the indigenous population manifests itself in rather a different way – by the presence, in a strictly Dacian context, of objects of proven Celtic make, datable to the first half of the third century BC. These are: two *Dux*-type fibulae of bronze wire, similar to the one I discovered in the Geto-Dacian site at Govora, in north Oltenia, and the baked clay cauldron found in the lower level of the well-known Getian *oppidum* at Tinosu. Other finds made at Sărata Monteoru attest the presence of Celtic cultural elements in a context which was already La Tène in type. At Glăvăneştii Vechi (Moldavia), however, numerous sherds of wheel-made ware of a reddish fabric, associated with indigenous Hallstatt pottery, were found. Under one large potsherd were the remains of an iron fibula still in the La Tène II traditional style. At the same site two graves were unearthed, one a cremation burial and the other an interment. By the skeleton's feet was a tubular iron ring, typically Celtic, but derived from a Hallstatt model. Chronologically these finds are attributable to the early phase of La Tène III, although in structure this equipment retains elements belonging to period II; this is a phenomenon which has been observed at other sites. Thus when the Celts arrived east of the Carpathians, the local Thracian culture was not yet fully developed. In fact in this area the Hallstatt persisted until the turn of the fourth century BC.

After the first incursion of the Celtic warriors, their cultural influence made itself felt through the peaceful and reciprocal relationship that was established between the two peoples.

Evidence for the first Celtic horizon in Transylvania comes almost entirely from warriors' graves. The tomb of Silivaș on the Mureș, near Aiud belongs to this early series of graves. It was discovered completely by chance and contained a Celtic
Fig. 67 sword, the chape of a scabbard, an Italian-type iron helmet with a knob on top, two iron spearheads, a curved sabre also of iron (*sica*), an iron knife-dagger, and an iron fibula which, although of a La Tène II design, can be attributed chronologically to La Tène IIIa. This grave furniture in general dates from about 300 BC. At this site were recovered from time to time various objects that had come from disturbed grave deposits, among them pottery, tools (shears); personal ornaments (*e.g.* bracelets, some with a tapered end for fitting into the other enlarged end, and numerous fragments of necklaces), weapons (knife-daggers), bridle-bits, and applied ornaments in foil bronze. A report from 1860 refers to an inhumation grave, while other accounts imply that the bodies in this same cemetery had been cremated. The tomb discovered there in 1938 contained a cremation burial. Evidence to date in Romania thus confirms that for the Celts this was a period of transition from interment to cremation, the latter practice being one they adopted from the indigenous population. The urnfield at Me-
Plate 73 diaș, and that discovered in 1963 at Ciumești, as well as the funerary urns, often covered by lids, at Dipșa (Transylvania) and those from south-west Oltenia all betray similar influences. No Celtic tumulus graves have yet been found in Romania. In general, grave furniture is unpretentious, but one cremation tomb at Ciumești (Maramureș) yielded rich goods (unpublished

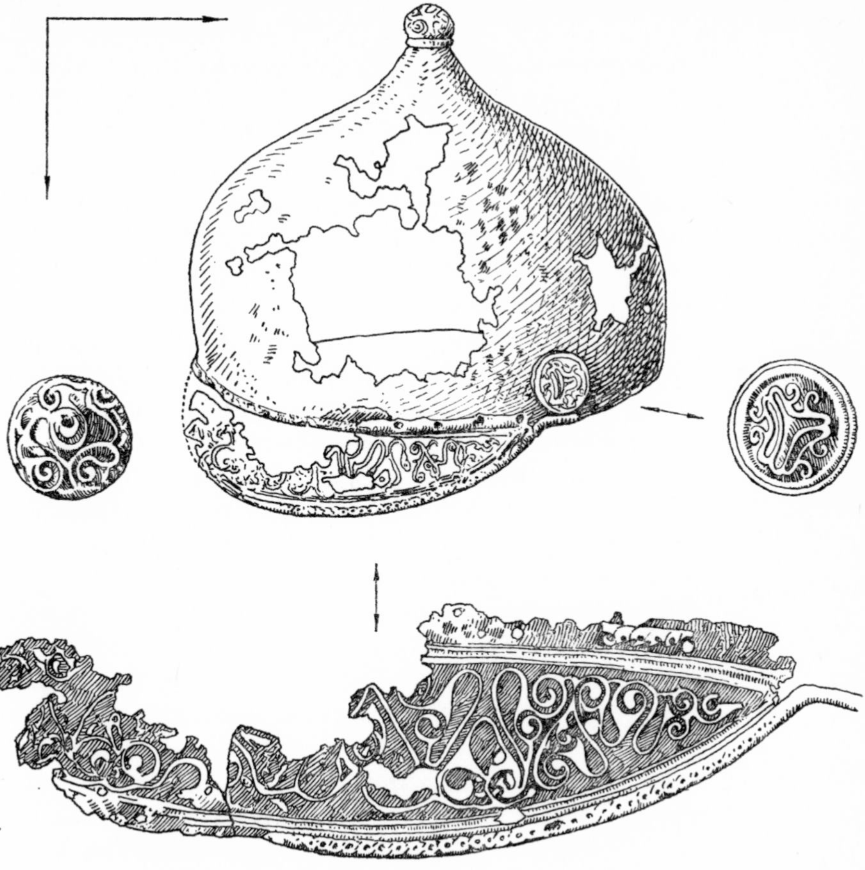

a

Fig. 67. a, Celtic helmet from Silivaș of the La Tène III period. b, Celtic weapons from Aiud

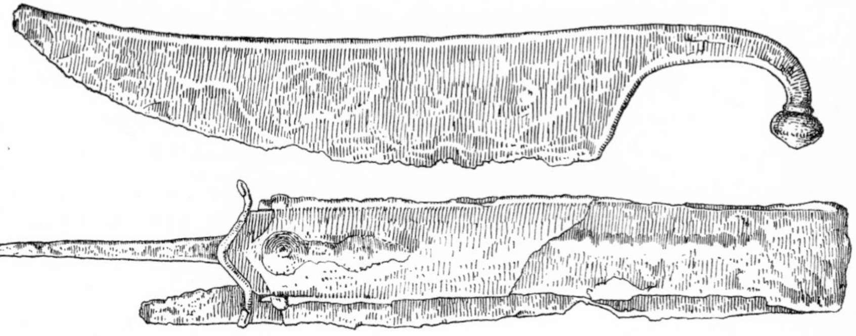

b

in Museum at Cluj. These included an iron helmet surmounted by an eagle with outstretched wings, artistically worked in bronze plaques, a coat of mail and two bronze greaves. This Ciumeşti helmet is the second Celtic example to be found in Romania. The largest cremation cemetery at present known in Romania is at Apahida, not far from Cluj, where 21 graves were excavated. Amongst the material so far recovered is the distinctive Celtic turned pottery; whole or broken fibulae, some of the *Dux* type in La Tène II style; bracelets composed of semi-ovoid elements; pieces of shields and swords; iron spear-heads, knife-daggers; iron rings, scissors and the like. To judge by its contents the Apahida cemetery post-dates the earliest Celtic antiquities in Romania.

Fig. 68

Other Celtic finds in Transylvania – from sites located between the Apuseni mountains and the east and south Carpathians – belong partly to phase IIIa and partly to phase IIIb. Some Celtic remains, providing evidence of cultural links between the Dacians and the Celtic centres of culture near Geto-Dacian territory, date from the last phase of La Tène IV. In Oltenia, such finds from all parts of the province testify to these three horizons.

Celtic culture in Romania is characterized by well-defined basic elements. Even coins have been found (for example, those of the Biatec or the Nonnos type), though the striking of coins by the Dacians cannot be related to the Celtic minting of money. Celtic painted ware also has been discovered.

Finds at Rast, Ciumeşti, Monteoru, Glăvăneştii Vechi, and elsewhere raise the important question of the nature of the relationship that existed between the Dacians and the Celts; a number of Celtic tombs contained curved sabres (*sica* type), and on Dacian sites distinctive Celtic material has been recovered. Recent Romanian archaeological data confirm that a Daco-Celtic cultural symbiosis took place in areas where the two populations lived together until the Celts were assimilated

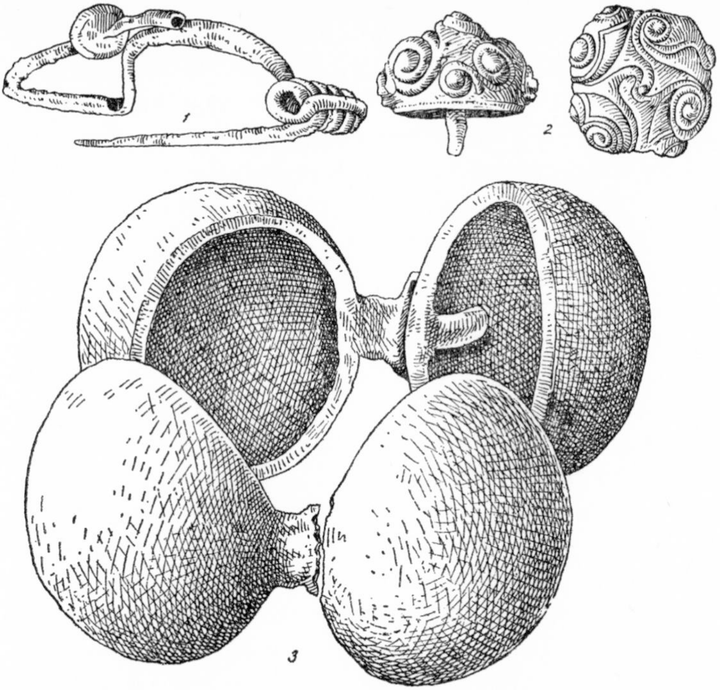

Fig. 68. Celtic ornaments. 1, 3, from the Apahìda cemetery; 2, from a grave at Cristurul Săcuiesc

by the local people as well as in areas where the cultural contact lasted longer owing to the existence, on the edge of the Geto-Dacian world, of Celtic centres, such as those of the Scordistae and the Boïans. There can be little doubt that the Celts coming into contact with the Geto-Dacians were in turn influenced by the latter.

The Bastarnes This people of German origin emigrated south and settled in northern and central Moldavia, where rich archaeological material, gathered after the Second World War, attests their presence. Other finds were made east of the Prut, in the Moldavian S.S.R. The discoveries at Poienești, a site in the Jassy region, deserve special mention; it was here that a cremation cemetery dating from the second and first centuries BC was excavated. The urns, made of a black ware are pear-shaped; they have small cross-shaped handles and the slightly everted rim is facetted on the inside. Also found were, among other things, bronze and iron fibulae, iron buckles and transparent glass beads with a gold leaf in the centre. Stock-breeding formed the basis of the Bastarnes' economic life, while quite a large number of Rhodian amphorae in the archaeological context of this people indicates that they were in commercial contact with the Hellenistic world. The Bastarnes came into conflict with the Geto-Dacians when they penetrated the territories inhabited by the latter, as various references in classical texts make clear. Justin-Trogus (XXXII, 3, 16), for example, relates how Oroles, head of a native Dacian unit, struggled against the Bastarnes about 200 BC. Likewise Rhemaxos, chieftain of another Dacian tribal association in Muntenia and south Moldavia, is mentioned in literary sources; it was to him, about 180 BC, that the town of Histria appealed for help against the threatened attach of Zoltes, the Thracian chieftain. In this connection, it should be emphasized that close political and economic links existed between the Thraco-Getians and the Greek towns near the Black Sea, during the period from Dromichaïtes to Burébista, the native 'kings' becoming the 'protectors' of these urban centres.

THE GETO-DACIAN CIVILIZATION BEFORE BURÉBISTA

The crystallization and diffusion of the La Tène culture in the Geto-Dacian territory of the Carpathians and the Danube was completed before the time of Burébista; it was during the third and second centuries BC that this process, to which the Celtic element contributed, took place. Iron metallurgy, based on the working of local ore deposits, spread throughout Romania and the adoption of the iron ploughshare led to a great expansion in agriculture. There is evidence that, in addition to the traditional types of tools, weapons and ornaments, various contributions from other cultures spread among the Geto-Dacians, though they had been adapted to conform with the tradition and to suit the needs and tastes of the latter. The potter's wheel was widely employed from La Tène III onwards, and everywhere in Geto-Dacian territory the potter's craft was based on this invention. Greek pottery forms were imitated, although the traditional Dacian hand-worked ware still retained an important place. Among characteristic pots still hand-moulded were the biconical skillet which persisted even into the post-La Tène period. The influence exerted by the Hallstatt elements was still marked. Local workshops, such as those of the oppidum at Popești-on-Argeș, made imitations of the best Greek ware involving specialized technological knowledge. Delian bowls with a decoration in relief, large storage jars and tiles, all produced by the local inhabitants, have been found. Plates 65-69

Before Burébista's time the Geto-Dacians created a novel art in silver-work, the good taste and mastery applied to which are attested by numerous treasures and isolated finds. These include various pieces of jewellery and silver luxury vessels such as those at Sîncrăieni, in Transylvania. During this period the Thracian fibula, a type which the south Thracians first made, was undergoing continuous development. Although the natives adopted the Celtic type of fibula, they also created a novel form – the Dacian knobbed fibula, usually in silver. Various bracelets were also made, for example, those with serpent-headed terminals, as well as necklaces of different kinds. Plates 70, 71 *Fig. 69*

Dacian Coins Coins represent another aspect of the standard of living and culture of the Geto-Dacians, who in fact possessed their own independent silver coinage. The Dacian coins were entirely original, with technical and stylistic features unlike those of Celtic coins. Since Celts penetrated only a part of the territories occupied by the Geto-Dacians, and that not until about 300 BC, their influence could have affected the issue of Dacian coins only west of the Carpathians and there only after that date. Owing to the relations they continuously main- Plate 72

Plate 72

tained with the southern Thracians and the Greek and Hellenistic south, the Geto-Dacians were able to borrow from the Greeks and southern Thracians the technique of minting coins. It may well be that the Geto-Dacians influenced the Celtic coinage, rather than the reverse, particularly where the 'eastern' group of Celtic coins are concerned. Dacian coins are a distinctive feature of the Dacian La Tène civilization, both as objects of intrinsic value and as a medium of exchange; they reflect an advanced stage in Geto-Dacian social and economic development. A first series of Dacian coins imitates the tetradrachms of Philip II of Macedon. Another series, distributed mainly south of the Carpathians, in the Getian zone, takes the form of imitations of the tetradrachm of Alexander the Great. A third group consists of a hybrid type of Geto-Dacian coin, resulting from a combination of the two above-mentioned series. There are yet other coins, some imitating those of Alexander Arrhides, others issued by the Greek towns, such as the Dacian silver coin copied from the tetradrachm of the town of Larissa. It was to meet the needs of internal trade that the coin was introduced among the Geto-Dacians in the third century BC. These coins did not circulate outside Geto-Dacian territories and each type, limited to a precise geographical zone, corresponded to the area belonging to any one tribal union. Several different monetary types have been identified and these have been conventionally, and no doubt provisionally, named the Vîrteju type in Muntenia, the Hunedoara type in Transylvania, the Huși type in Moldavia, the Amphipolis and Dobrești types in Oltenia, and so on. In Dobrudja, Moskon coins have been found that are datable to the beginning of the third or even the last years of the fourth century BC. The Geto-Dacian coins were also abundantly distributed in the second century, but at the beginning of the first this people ceased to mint coins, the local coinage being replaced by the Roman denarius which was now universally circulated. The disap-

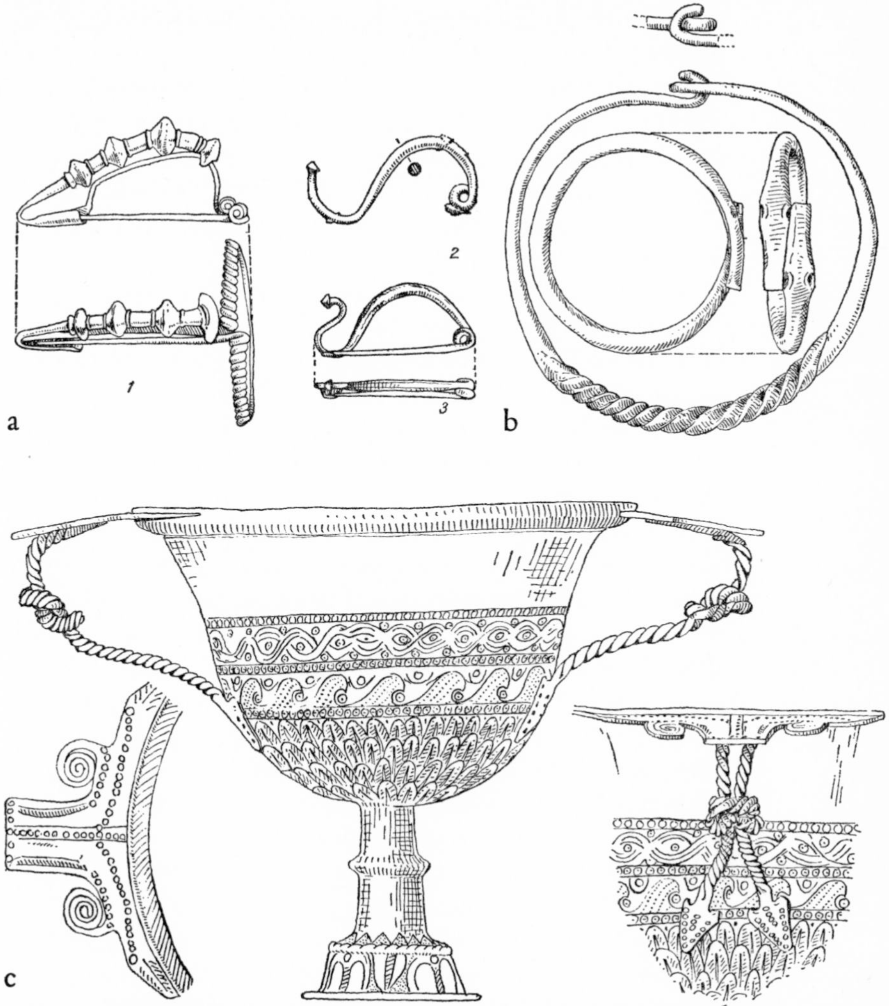

Fig. 69. a, Geto-Dacian La Tène objects. Silver knobbed-fibula from Intorsura (Oltenia) (1). Length, 10.6cm. Thracian bronze fibula from Bucharest (2). Length, 4.2cm. Thracian-type silver fibula from Oltenia (3). Length, 7.3cm. b, Getian ornaments from the Slimnic hoard (Transylvania). Silver torque and silver bangle with stylized animal-head terminals. Diameter of torque, 12.5cm., bangle to scale. c, Decorated silver pedestalled cup from the Dacian treasure at Sîncrăieni. Height, about 12.8cm.

pearance of Dacian coins, whose circulation was restricted to the tribal unions, corresponds to the uprising of the Geto-Dacians under Burébista, chief of a political organization far larger than those of the past and possessing the character of an emergent state based on slavery. It was against this political and economic background that a single unit of money became necessary, and this monetary function was performed by the denarius of the Roman Republic.

In the first century BC the Dacians began counterfeiting the Roman denarius – but it is impossible to distinguish the counterfeit coin from the Roman original. In 1961, at the Dacian fortress of Tilișca, in the Sibiu district, 14 moulds were discovered that had served for striking the denarius, perfectly imitated by the local engravers. This city was abandoned at the time of Burébista.

Large numbers of Dacian coins have been recovered from coin hoards; they are also found associated with Dacian personal ornaments or with coins of Greek or Roman towns prior to the first century BC. In circulation alongside the local money used by the Geto-Dacians, and a sign of their economic prosperity, were Greek coins from various towns, including the Pontic towns of Histria, Callatis and Tomis; Macedonian coins, including those mentioned above and those belonging to Lysimachos; and Roman coins.

Oppidum Life and Integration There are attested Geto-Dacian sites from the fourth century BC, defended with earth ditches and ramparts. Fortified settlements (*oppida*) of this kind were called *davae* by the local population and *poleis* by Greek authors; they are mentioned for the first time on the occasion of the expeditions undertaken by Alexander the Great and Lysimachos. The excavations at Popești, Tinosul, Piscul Crăsani, Poiana and elsewhere have enabled us to form a clearer picture of them. They were, in fact, economic, military, political and religious centres, with a function similar for the most part to that of the real urban centres of the ancient civilizations, although they were in general more rustic in appearance.

Recent excavations have thrown new light upon the prosperous *oppidum* life which was developing in the Danubian-Pontic zone. When Roman influence was just beginning to make itself felt, in the second century BC, the Geto-Dacian La Tène culture was in the process of coordinating its individual elements, with all their distinctive and original features.

Burébista The social and economic development of the Geto-Dacians reached its peak a little after 100 BC. There was marked progress in all walks of life and continuous development in the economic sphere led to an increasingly hierarchical society. Although local coinage played its part in this, it was soon replaced by Roman money within the emerging state which finally took form under Burébista, with the result that economic activity was stimulated throughout Geto-Dacian territory.

But the Geto-Dacians of Burébista's time and after will be the subject of a later volume in this series.

Postscriptum

At the suggestion of the General Editor, I am adding a few comments to the brief mention (on page 49) of the discovery of three clay tablets at Tărtăria, on the river Mureș, not far from Turdaș in Transylvania. These tablets were found in 1961 by N. Vlassa and published by him in 1964. Fired for purposes of preservation, they had been deposited in a small pit, indicating a magico-religious context, at a prehistoric site where the occupation levels of four successive cultures have been identified: the Criș, the Turdaș, the Petrești, and the Coțofeni. The pit forms part of the last horizon of the Turdaș layer.

As the excavations in central Transylvania and in particular those at Alba Iulia (Lumea Nouă) have established, the well-defined Turdaș culture spans the whole of the Middle Neolithic and ends when the Petrești painted-pottery culture comes into being. From a chronological and stratigraphical point of view it must be borne in mind that the pit containing the tablets is overlaid by the first horizon of the Petrești, while its contents, which included twenty-six idols, are characteristic of the final Turdaș horizon (Middle Neolithic) of Transylvania. In any case, neither the pit nor its contents could possibly be considered contemporary with Vinča A, and so enable a parallel to be drawn between the latter and the Mesopotamian region, as has recently been suggested in some quarters. The Tărtăria tablets bear markings that are familiar in sites of the Vinča-Turdaș complex and even the Criș. However, only five out of the twenty-four signs – according to A. Falkenstein – bear any resemblance to those of proto-historic Sumerian writing (Uruk III B).

Bearing in mind the over-all picture presented by the Criș, Vinča and Turdaș finds, and having regard to the particular nature of the Tărtăria tablets, I believe that the markings on these are more or less abstract signs unconnected with Sumerian influence or with 'scribes' who had reached the Danube from Mesopotamia, though contacts were undeniably established between that area and the Middle East in Early and Middle Neolithic times. The evaluation of such signs as 'writing' rests on a hypothesis which for the present is very difficult to substantiate.

D.B.

Bucharest, 4.6.67

Bibliography

Abbreviations:

Dacia	*Dacia, recherches et découvertes archéologiques en Roumanie*, Bucharest, I–XII, 1924–1947; New Series (N.S.), I–VIII, 1957–1964
MCA	*Materiale şi cercetări arheologice*
NEH	*Nouvelles études d'histoire, I, Présentées au Xe Congrès des Sciences Historiques*, Rome, 1955, Bucharest, 1955; II, *Publiées à l'occasion du XIe Congrès des Sciences Historiques*, Stockholm, 1960, Bucharest, 1960
SC	*Studii clasice*
SCIV	*Studii şi cercetări de istorie veche*
SCN	*Studii şi cercetări de numismatică*
*	Rumanian text with French and Russian resumé

GENERAL

ANDRIEŞESCU, ION, *Contribuţie la Dacia înainte de romani.* Iassy, 1912.

* BERCIU, DUMITRU. *L'Archéologie préhistorique de l'Olténie.* Craiova, 1939.

— and COMŞA, EUGEN. Săpăturile arheologice de la Balta Verde şi Gogoşu (1949 şi 1950). *MCA*, II, 1956, pp. 251–289.

—, *Zorile istoriei în Carpaţi şi la Dunăre.* Bucharest, 1966.

CONDURACHI, EMIL. Vingt années de recherches archéologiques en Roumanie (1944–1964). *Dacia*, N.S., VIII, 1964, pp. 5–37.

DAICOVICIU, CONSTANTIN. *La Transylvanie dans l'antiquité.* Bucharest, 1945.

Istoria României. Vol. I. Bucharest, 1960.

NESTOR, ION. Der Stand der Vorgeschichtsforschung in Rumänien. Sonderabdruck aus dem *22. Bericht der römisch-germanischen Kommission*, 1933.

* PÂRVAN, VASILE. *Getica. Une protohistoire de la Dacie.* Bucharest, 1926.

* —, *Dacia. Civilizaţiile străvechi din reguinile carpato-danubiene.* Bucharest, 1958.

PIPPIDI, D. M. *Contribuţii la istoria veche a României.* Bucharest, 1958.

—, and BERCIU, DUMITRU. *Din istoria Dobrogei. Geţi si Greci la Dună-*

rea de Jos din cele mai vechi timpuri pînă la cucerirea romană. Vol. I. Bucharest, 1965.

SCHROLLER, H. *Die Stein-und Kupferzeit Siebenbürgens.* Berlin, 1933.

VULPE, RADU. *Histoire ancienne de la Dobroudja.* Bucharest, 1938.

—, *Izvoare. Les fouilles de 1936–1948.* Bucharest, 1957.

THE PALAEOLITHIC

* BITIRI, MARIA. Considération sur le début du paléolithique supérieur en Roumanie. *SCIV,* 16, no. 1, 1965, pp. 5–16.

NICOLĂESCU-PLOPŞOR, C. S. Le paléolithique en Roumanie. *Dacia,* V–VI, 1935–1936, pp. 41–107.

—, Le paléolithique dans la République Populaire Roumaine à la lumière des dernières recherches. *Dacia,* N.S., I, 1957, pp. 41–60.

—, Sur la présence du swidérien en Roumanie. *Dacia,* N.S., II, 1958, pp. 5–38.

—, and MOROŞAN, I.N. Sur le commencement du paléolithique en Roumanie. *Dacia,* N.S., III, 1959, pp. 9–33.

—, Das Paläolithikum in Rumänien. *Archaeologia Austriaca,* 31, 1962, pp. 74–95.

PĂUNESCU, ALEXANDRU. Perjitki tardenuazskoi kulturî v drevnem neolite v Ciumeşti. *Dacia,* N.S., VII, 1964, pp. 467–475.

THE NEOLITHIC

BERCIU, DUMITRU. Une civilisation néolithique récemment découverte en Roumanie: la civilisation de Hamangia. *NEH* I, 1955, pp. 29–46.

—, Chronologie relative du Néolithique du Bas-Danube, à la lumière des nouvelles fouilles faites en Roumanie. *Actes du Symposion International de Prague, d'octobre, 1959, L'Europe à la fin de l'âge de la pierre,* Prague, 1961, pp. 101–124.

* —, *Contributions aux problèmes du néolithique en Roumanie, à la lumière des nouvelles fouilles.* Bucharest, 1961.

—, Deux chefs-d'œuvre de l'art néolithique en Roumanie: le 'couple' de la civilisation de Hamangia. *Dacia,* N.S., IV, 1960, pp. 423–441.

CANTACUZINO, GHEORGHE and MORINTZ, SEBASTIAN. Die jungsteinzeitlichen Funde in Cernica (Bukarest). *Dacia,* N.S., VII, 1963, pp. 27–89.

COMŞA, EUGEN. Quelques données relatives à la périodisation et à l'évolution de la civilisation de Boian. *Dacia,* N.S., I, 1957, pp. 61–72.

—, Betrachtungen über die Linearbandkeramik auf dem Gebiet der rumänischen Volksrepublik und der angrenzenden Länder. *Dacia*, N.S., III, 1959, pp. 35–57.

—, Contribution à l'historique des rites funéraires de l'époque néolithique sur le territoire roumain. *Omagiu lui Constantin Daicoviciu*, 1960, pp. 83–106.

—, Nouvelles données relatives à l'évolution des civilisations néolithiques sur le territoire de la Roumanie. *NEH*, II, 1960, pp. 7–17.

Dinu, M. K voprosu o kulture sarovidnîh amfor na territorii Moldovî. *Dacia*, N.S., IV, 1960, pp. 89–106.

Dumitrescu, Hortensia. La station préhistorique de Horodiştea sur le Pruth. *Dacia*, IX–X, 1941–1944, pp. 127–163.

* —, Contribution au problème de l'origine de la civilisation précucuténienne. *SCIV*, 8, no. 1–4, 1957, pp. 53–73.

—, Découvertes concernant un rite funéraire magique dans l'aire de la civilisation de la céramique peinte du type Cucuteni-Tripolje. *Dacia*, N.S., I, 1957, pp. 97–116.

Dumitrescu, Vladimir. Rapière en bronze du type mycénien trouvée au sud-ouest de Bucarest (près Roşiorii-de-Vede). *Dacia*, V–VI, 1935–1936, pp. 169–173.

—, *et al. Hăbăşeşti. Monografie arheologică.* Bucharest, 1954.

—, La station préhistorique de Hăbăşeşti et quelques-uns des problèmes de la civilisation Cucuteni-Tripolje. *Památky archaeologické, Praha*, 59, no. 1, 1958, pp. 265–296.

—, Origine et évolution de la civilisation Cucuteni-Tripolje. *Archeologia, Varsovie*, 13, 1963, pp. 1–40.

Falkenstein, A., Zu den Tontafeln aus Tărtăria, in *Germania*, 43, 1965, pp. 269–273.

Mateescu, Corneliu. La plus ancienne phase de la civilisation de Vădastra, Vădastra I, à la lumière des nouvelles fouilles de Vădastra. *Bericht über den V. Internationalen Kongress für Vor- und Frühgeschichte*, Hamburg, 1958. Berlin, 1961, pp. 529–534.

—, Principaux résultats des nouvelles fouilles de Vădastra. *Archeologické rozhledy*, 14, no. 3, 1962, pp. 404–420.

—, Contribution à l'étude de la civilisation de Vădastra: phase II (d'après les nouvelles fouilles de Vădastra). *Atti del VI Congresso Internazionale delle Scienze Preistoriche e Protostoriche*, Rome, 1965, pp. 258–263.

Milojčić, Vl., Die Tontafeln von Tărtăria (Siebenbürgen) und die absolute Chronologie des mitteleuropäischen Neolithikums, in *Germania*, 43, 1965, pp. 261-268.

* Necrasov, Olga. Considérations sur les populations de l'âge de la pierre et du commencement de l'âge des métaux du territoire de la République Populaire Roumaine. *Omagiu lui Constantin Daicoviciu,* 1960, pp. 415–429.

Nestor, Ion. Zur Periodisierung der späteren Zeitstufen des Neolithikums in der Rumänischen Volksrepublik. *Dacia,* N.S., IV, 1960, pp. 53–68.

Petrescu-Dîmboviţa, M. Nouvelles données concernant le néolithique carpatho-balkanique. *Balcania,* VIII, 1945, pp. 192–215.

* —, Date noi privind înmormîntările cu ocru în Moldova. *SCIV,* 2, no. 1, 1950, pp. 110–123.

—, Die wichtigsten Ergebnisse der archäologischen Ausgrabungen in der neolithischen Siedlung von Truşeşti (Moldau). *Prähistorische Zeitschrift,* 41, 1963, pp. 172–186.

Schmidt, Hubert. *Cucuteni in der oberen Moldau.* Berlin, Leipzig, 1932.

Vlassa, Nicolae. Chronology of the neolithic in Transylvania, in the light of the Tărtăria Settlement's stratigraphy. *Dacia,* N.S., 1963, VII, pp. 485–494.

* Vulpe, Alexandru. Sur la chronologie des haches doubles en cuivre à tranchants opposés. *SCIV,* 15, no. 4, 1964, p. 457–466.

Vulpe, Radu. Civilisation précucuténienne récemment découverte à Izvoare, en Moldavie. *Eurasia septentrionalis antiqua,* XI, 1937, pp. 134–146

Zaharia, Eugenia. Considérations sur la civilisation de Criş à la lumière des sondages de Leţ. *Dacia,* N.S., VI, 1962, pp. 5–51.

Zirra, Vlad. Kultura pogrebenii s ohroi v zakarpatskih oblastiah RNR. *Materialî i issledovaniia po arheologhii SSSR,* Chisnău, 1960, pp. 97–127.

THE BRONZE AGE

Andrieşescu, Ion. *Asupra epocii de bronz în România.* I. *Un depou de bronz la Sinaia;* II. *Obiecte de bronz de la Predeal.* Bucharest, 1916.

* —, Piscul Crăsani. Les découvertes archéologiques pendant l'été du 1923. *Memoriile Secţiei Istorice a Academiei Române,* ser. 3, vol. III, 1924, pp. 113–851.

* Aricescu, Andrei. Les dépôts de pièces en bronze de Dobrogea. *SCIV,* 16, no. 1, 1965, pp. 17–42

Berciu, Dumitru. Sur les débuts de l'âge du bronze au Bas-Danube. *Dacia,* N.S., VIII, 1964, pp. 313–318.

—, Quelques données préliminaires concernant la civilisation de Cerna-voda. *Slovenská Archeologia,* 12, no. 1, 1964, pp. 269–280.

—, Die Verbicioara-Kultur. Vorbericht über eine neue in Rumänien entdeckte bronzezeitliche Kultur. *Dacia,* N.S., V, 1961, pp. 123–161.

Dumitrescu, Vladimir. Quelques observations au sujet des civilisations danubiennes des champs d'urnes de l'âge du bronze. *NEH,* II, 1960, pp. 19–30.

* —, *La nécropole d'incinération de l'âge du bronze de Cîrna.* Bucharest, 1961.

—, and Stratan, Ion. Keramik der Vučedol-Kultur aus Moldova Veche im Banat. *Dacia,* N.S., VI, 1962, pp. 411–427.

Dunăreanu-Vulpe, EC. La nécropole de l'âge du bronze de Poiana. *Dacia,* V–VI, 1935–1936, pp. 151–167.

* Florescu, A. C. Contributions à la connaissance de la civilisation de Noua. *Arheologia Moldovei,* II–III, 1964. pp. 143–216.

* Florescu, Marilena. Contributions à la problème du commencement de l'âge du bronze en Moldavie. *Arheologia Moldovei,* II–III, 1964, pp. 105–125.

* —, Quelques observations concernant l'évolution du bronze ancien en Moldavie. *SCIV,* 16, no. 4, 1965, pp. 649–661.

Horedt, Kurt. Siebenbürgen und Mykenä. *NEH,* II, 1960, pp. 31–44.

—, Die Wietenbergkultur. *Dacia,* N.S., IV, 1960, pp. 107–137.

Leahu, Valeriu, *Cultura Tei,* Bucharest, 1966.

Nestor, Ion. Étude sur l'exploitation préhistorique du cuivre en Roumanie. Le dépôt de barres-colliers de Deva. *Dacia,* IX–X, 1941–1944, pp. 165–181.

—, Sur les débuts de la métallurgie du cuivre et du bronze en Roumanie. *NEH,* I, 1955, pp. 47–63.

Ordentlich, Ivan. Poselenia v Otomani v svete poslednih raskopok. *Dacia,* N.S., VII, 1963, p. 115–138.

Popescu, Dorin. La tombe à ocre de Casimcea. *Dacia,* VII–VIII, 1937–1940, pp. 85–91.

—, *Die frühe und mittlere Bronzezeit in Siebenbürgen,* Bucharest, 1944.

—, Einige Bemerkungen zur Bronzezeit Siebenbürgens. *Acta Archaeologica,* no. 7, 1956.

* —, À propos de quelques trésors d'objets en or de l'âge du bronze. *SCIV* 12, no. 2, 1962, pp. 399–414.

PROX, ALFRED. *Die Schneckenbergkultur.* Kronstadt, 1941.

ROSETTI, DINU. *Die Bukarester Kultur.* Bucharest, 1936.

VULPE, ALEXANDRU. K voprosu o periodizaţii bronzovogo veka v Moldove. *Dacia,* N.S., V, 1961, pp. 105–123.

ZAHARIA, EUGENIA. Das Gräberfeld von Balinteşti Cioinagi und einige Fragen der Bronzezeit in der Moldau. *Dacia,* N.S., VII, 1963, pp. 139–176.

THE HALLSTATT IRON AGE

ALEXANDRESCU, PETRE and EFTIMIE, VICTORIA. Tombes thraces d'époque archaique dans la nécropole tumulaire d'Histria. *Dacia,* N.S., III, 1959, pp. 143–164.

ANDRIEŞESCU ION. Nouvelles contributions sur l'âge du bronze en Roumanie. Le dépôt de bronzes de Drajna de Jos et l'épée de Bucium. *Dacia,* II, 1925, pp. 345–384.

* BERCIU, DUMITRU. Une découverte thraco-scythique en Dobrogea et le problème scythique du Bas-Danube. *SCIV,* 10, no. 1, 1959, pp. 7–48.

—, Neue scythische Funde aus Rumänien und Bulgarien. *Prähistorische Zeitschrift,* 41, 1963, pp. 190–198.

DÖRNER, EGON. Der Goldfund von Sîntana-Arad. *Dacia,* N.S., IV, 1960, pp. 471–479.

HOREDT, KURT. Skifskie nahodki v Komlode. *Dacia,* N.S., IV, 1960, pp. 481–488.

—, Hallstättische Tierfiguren aus Lechinţa de Mureş (Rayon Luduş). *Dacia,* N.S., VII, 1963, pp. 527–534.

MORINTZ, SEBASTIAN. Navaia galştatskaia gruppa v Moldove. *Dacia,* N.S., I, 1957, pp. 117–132.

NESTOR, ION. Ein Bronzedepot aus Moigrad (Rumänien). *Prähistorische Zeitschrift,* 26, no. 1–2, 1935, pp. 24–57.

PETRESCU-DÎMBOVIŢA, M. Cetăţuia de la Stoicani. *MCA,* I, 1954, pp. 13–211.

—, Koneţ bronzovogo i naciale rannejeleznogo veka v Moldove v svete poslednih arheologhiceskih raskopok. *Dacia,* N.S., IV, 1960, pp. 139–159.

Popa, Al. and Berciu, Ion Contributions à l'étude des dépôts d'objets hallstattiens. *Dacia,* N.S., VIII, 1964, pp. 87–100.

Rusu, Mircea. 'Dokimmeriiskie' detali konskoi sbruii iz Transilvanii. *Dacia,* N.S., IV, 1960, pp. 161–180.

—, Die Verbreitung der Bronzehorte in Transilvanien von Ende der Bronzezeit bis in die Mittlere Hallstattzeit. *Dacia,* N.S., VII, 1963, pp. 177–210.

Vulpe, Alexandru. Voprosî v sviazi s konțom rannejeleznogo veka v svete raskopok v Feridjele. *Dacia,* N.S., IV, 1960, pp. 181–199.

THE LA TÈNE IRON AGE

Berciu, Dumitru. À propos de la genèse de la civilisation de Latène chez les géto-daces. *Dacia,* N.S., I, 1957, pp. 133–141.

—, Die Stellung der Geten im Lichte der Archäologie. *Dacia,* N.S., V, 1961, pp. 163–184.

* Bichir, Gheorghe. Observations sur les nécropoles du type Poienești de Moldavie et les rapports de celles-ci avec le monde sarmate. *SCIV,* 12, no. 2, 1961, pp. 253–271.

* —, Nouvelle contribution à la connaissance de la civilisation matérielle des carpes. *SCIV,* 16, no. 4, 1965, pp. 675–694.

Daicoviciu, Constantin. Problema continuității în Dacia. *Anuarul Institutului de Studii Clasice, Cluj,* III, 1936–1940, pp. 222–239.

— and Ferenczi, Al. *Așezările dacice din Munții Orăștiei.* Bucharest, 1951.

—, Studiul traiului dacilor în Munții Orăștiei. *SCIV,* 2, no. 1, 1951, pp. 95–127.

* —, *La forteresse dace de Piatra Roșie. Monographie archéologique,* Bucharest, 1954.

—, Le problème de l'état et de la culture des daces à la lumière des nouvelles recherches. *NEH,* I, 1955, pp. 121–137.

Daicoviciu, Hadrian. Il tempio-calendario dacico di Sarmizegetusa. *Dacia,* N.S., IV, 1960, pp. 231–254.

—, *Dacii.* Bucharest, 1965.

Dörner, Egon. Römerzeitliche dakische Brandgräber aus Sîntana-Arad. *Omagiu lui Constantin Daicoviciu,* 1960, pp. 155–159.

FLOCA, OCTAVIAN. *Contribuţii la cunoaşterea tezaurelor de argint dacice.* Bucharest, 1956.

LUPU, NICOLAE. Die Münze in der dakischen Burg von Tilişca. *Forschungen zur Volks- und Landeskunde,* 7, no. 1, 1964, Sibiu.

* MACREA, MIHAI. Burébista et les celtes du Moyen-Danube. *SCIV,* 7, no. 1–2, 1956, pp. 119–136.

—, and RUSU, MIRCEA. Der dakische Friedhof von Porolissum und das Problem der dakischen Bestattungsbräuche in der Spätlatènezeit. *Dacia,* N.S., IV, 1960, pp. 201–229.

MITREA, BUCUR. Penetrazione commerciale e circolazione monetaria nella Dacia prima della conquista. *Ephemeris Dacoromana,* X, 1945, pp. 1–152.

* —, Les relations commerciales des géto-daces de la Valachie avec la République Romaine, telles qu'elles ressortent des découvertes monétaires. *SCN,* II, 1958, pp. 123–238.

NESTOR, ION. Keltische Gräber bei Mediaş. Ein Beitrag zur Frage der frühen keltischer Funde in Siebenbürgen. *Dacia,* VII–VIII, 1937–1940, pp. 159–182.

PÂRVAN, VASILE. La pénétration hellénique et hellénistique dans la vallée du Danube. Académie Roumaine. *Bulletin de la Séction Historique, Bucarest,* X, 1923, pp. 23–47.

—, Considérations sur les sépultures celtiques de Gruia. *Dacia,* I, 1924, pp. 35–50.

* PIPPIDI, D. M. Istros et les Gétes au IIIe siècle av. notre ère. *SC,* III, 1961, pp. 53–66.

* PREDA, CONSTANTIN. Problèmes de numismatique géto-dace. *SCN,* III, 1960, pp. 43–79.

* —, Monnaies d'un type inconnue provenant de Dobrogea. *SCIV,* 15, no. 3, 1964, pp. 401–410

RUSU, MIRCEA. Depozitul de vase dacice de la Gusteriţa-Sibiu. *Studii şi cercetări stiinţifice, Cluj,* 6, no. 3–4, 1955.

VULPE, RADU. Le problème des bastarnes à la lumière des découvertes archéologiques en Moldavie. *NEH,* I, 1955, pp. 103–119.

—, La civilisation dace et ses problèmes à la lumière des dernières fouilles de Poiana, en Basse-Moldavie. *Dacia,* N.S., I, 1957, pp. 143–164.

—, Les gétes de la rive gauche du Bas-Danube et les romains. *Dacia,* N.S., IV, 1960, pp. 309–332.

Sources of Illustrations

Most of the photographs reproduced in the plates were supplied by courtesy of the museums where the objects are housed, and these institutions are named in the Notes on the Plates, where AIB stands for the Archaeological Institute in Bucharest. In other instances, the publication and/or author is indicated. Where no mention is made of the source, the photographs belong to the Author.

Apart from those enumerated below, the figures come from the following sources: *Dacia* N.S. I–VIII, 1957–64; *MCA* I–VIII, 154, 1962; SCIV I–XV, 1950–64 (authors: Alexandrescu, A.; Berciu, D.; Bitiri, M.; Crişan, H. I.; Dolinescu-Ferche, S.; Dumitrescu, H.; Dumitrescu, V.; Dănilă, S.; Horedt, K.; Mogoşan, F.; Morintz, S.; Nestor, I.; Nicolăescu-Plopşor, C.; Păunescu, A.; Petrescu-Dîmbovitza, M.; Popescu, D.; Vulpe, A.; Vulpe, R.; Zaharia, E.).

Fig. 13, after Berciu, D., *Cultura Hamangia* I, 1966; 14, courtesy Angelescu, N.; 16–17, 19(1), after Berciu, D., *Contribuţii*, 1961; 31, after Constantiniu, M. and Panait, I, in *Cercetări arheologice în Bucureşti* I, 1963; 32, 35, 50, after Popescu, D., *Die frühe und mittlere Bronzezeit in Siebenbürgen*, 1944; 34, after Dinu, M., in *Arheologia Moldovei* I, 1961; 37a, 53a, courtesy Mrs A. Alexandrescu; 41, 42(2), after Leahu, V., in *Cercetări arheologice în Burcureşti* I, 1963; 44, courtesy Mr R. Vulpe; 49, after Florescu, A., in *Arheologia Moldovei* II–III, 1964; 52, 53b–c, after Holste, F., *Hortfunde Südosteuropas*, 1951; 64, after Preda, F., in *Analele Universităţii Bucureşti, seria ştiinţe sociale, istorie* IX, 16, 1961; 67, 68, after Popescu, D., 'Celţii în Transilvania', in *Transilvania* 75, 1944; 8, 9, 22, Author's excavations with Purcărescu, P. and Petre, G.; 11, Author's excavations with Berciu, I.; 25, 27, 42(1), Author's excavations.

1

2

3

4

5

6

7

8

9

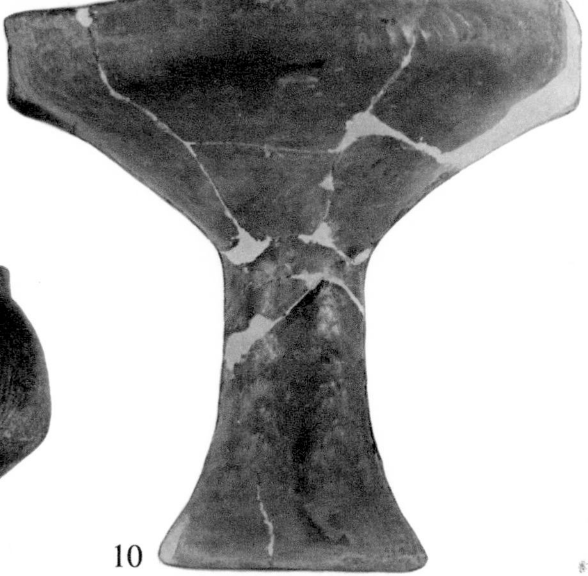

10

11

12

13

14

15

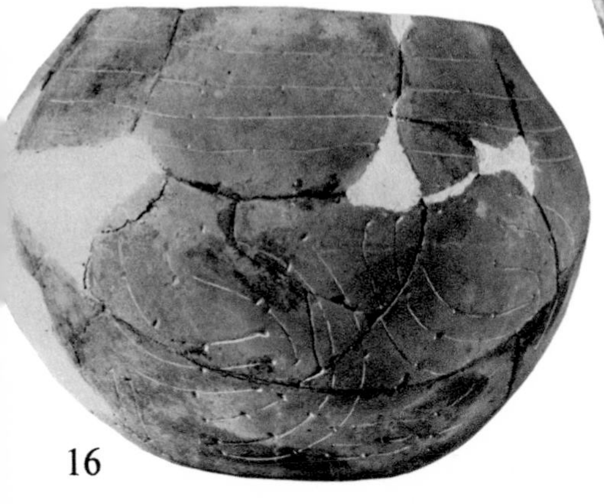

16

17

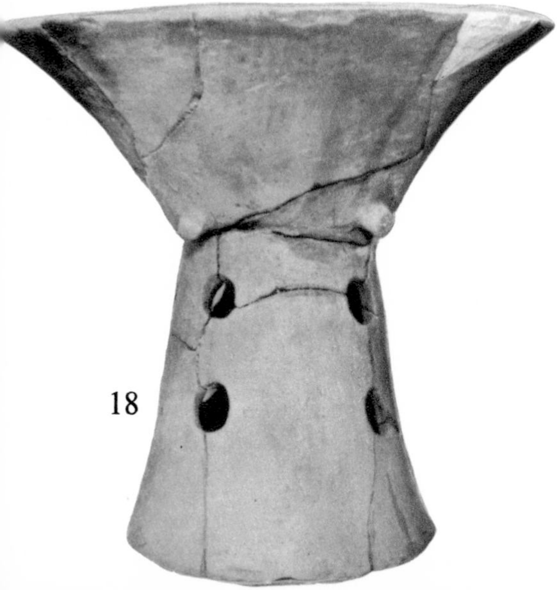

18

19

20

21

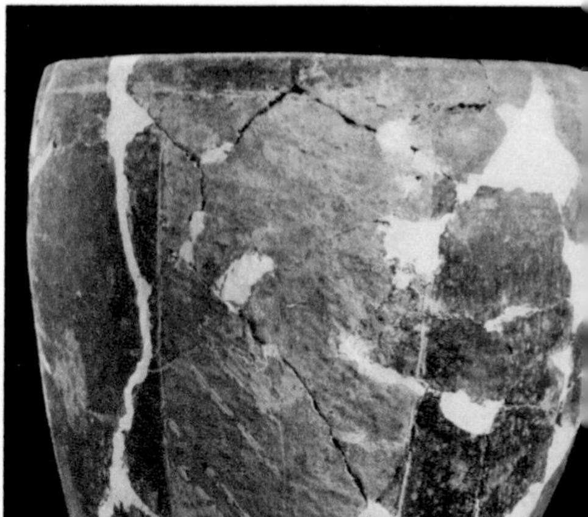

22

23

24

25

26

27

28

29

30

31a

31b

32

33

34

35

36

37

38

39

40

41

42

43

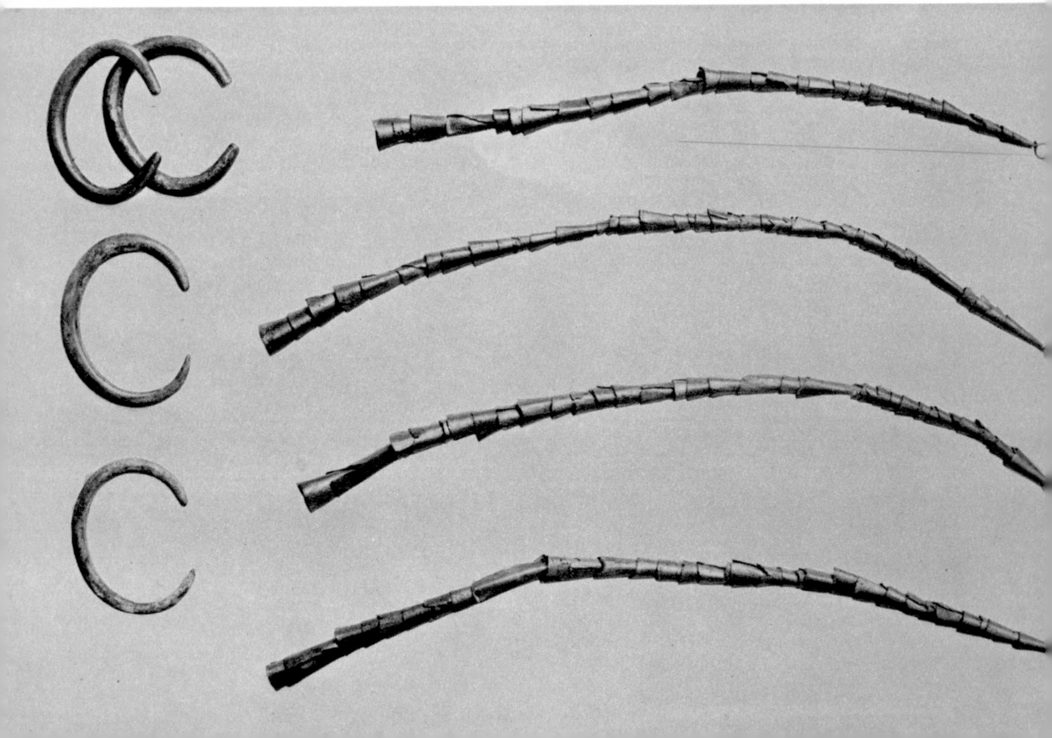

44

45

46

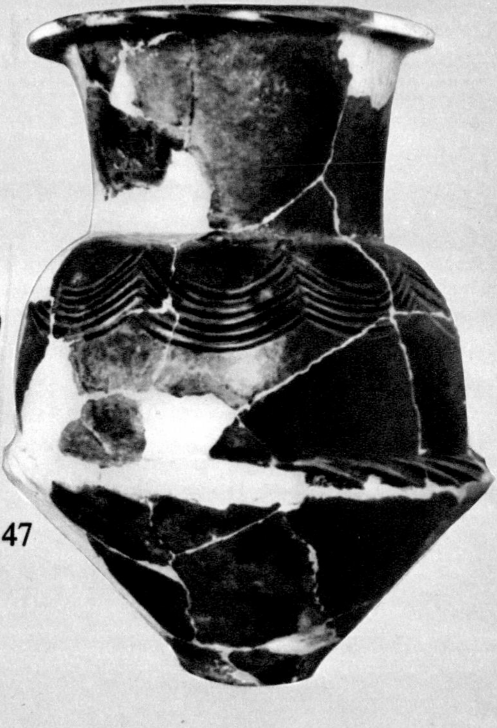

47

48

49

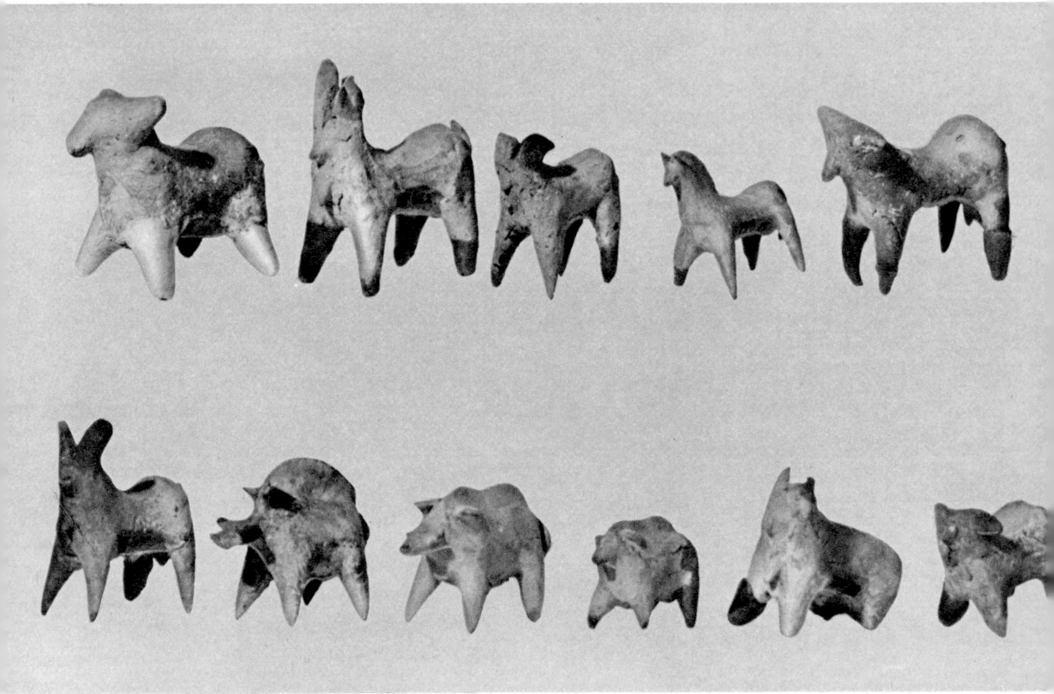

50

51

52

54

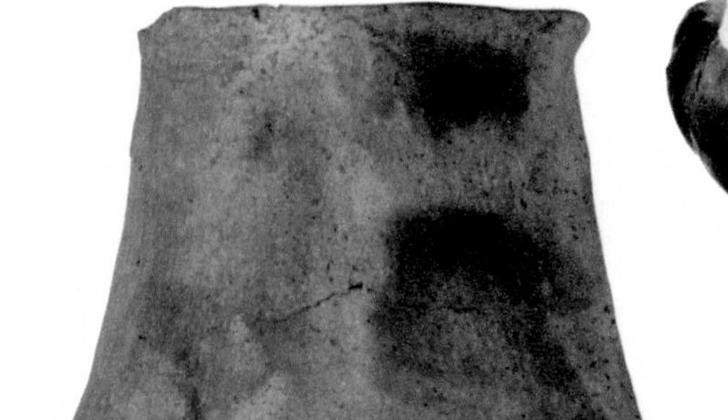

53

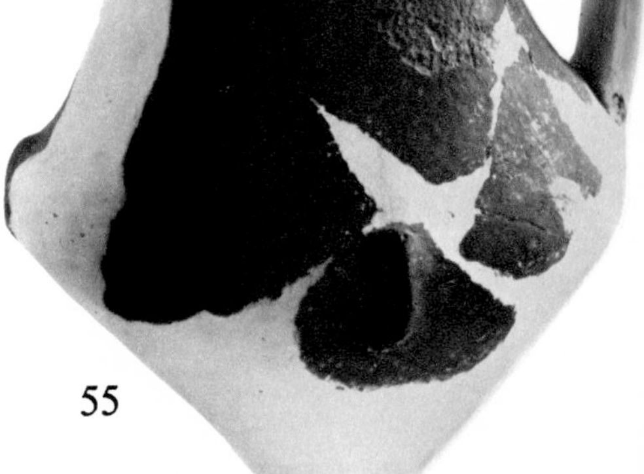

55

56

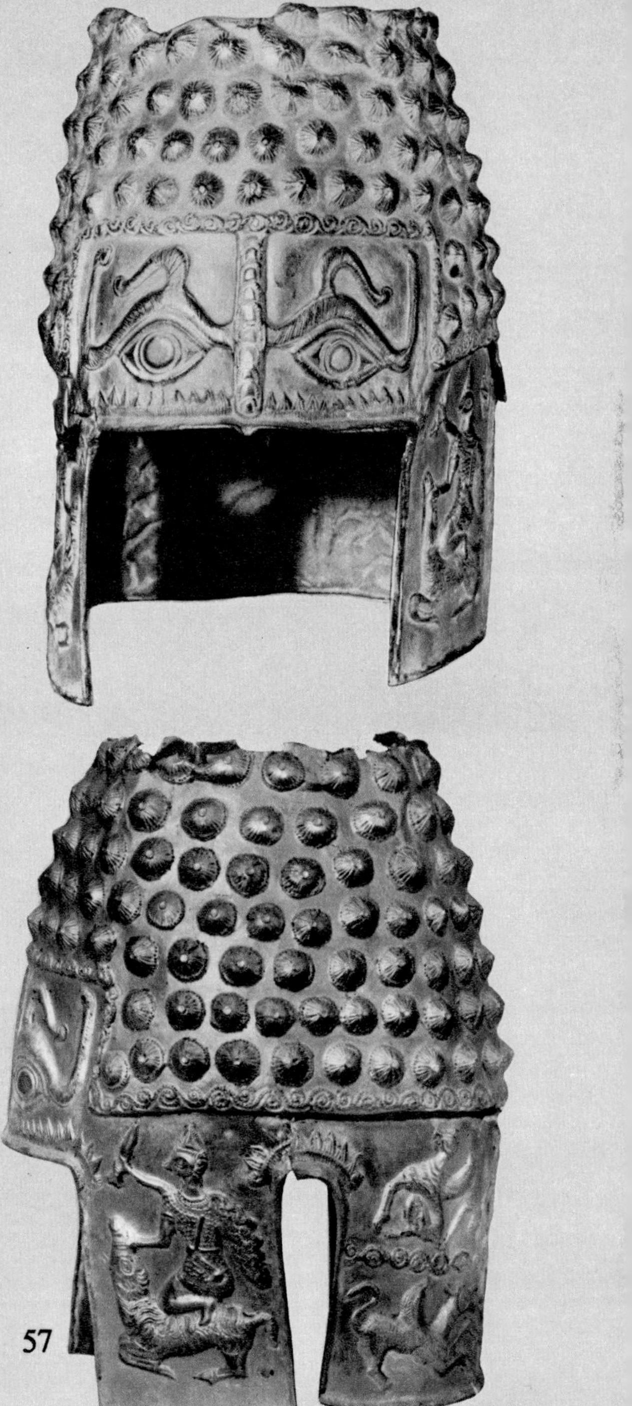

57

58

59

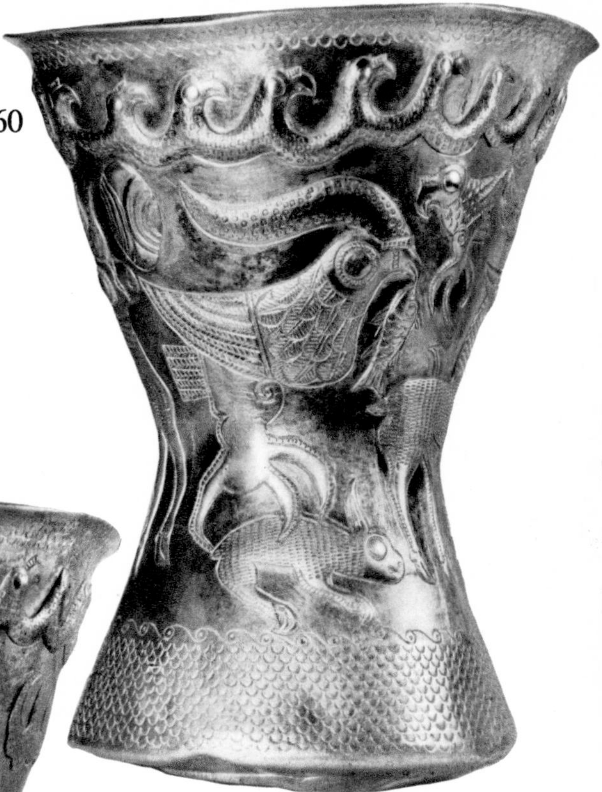
60

61

62–64

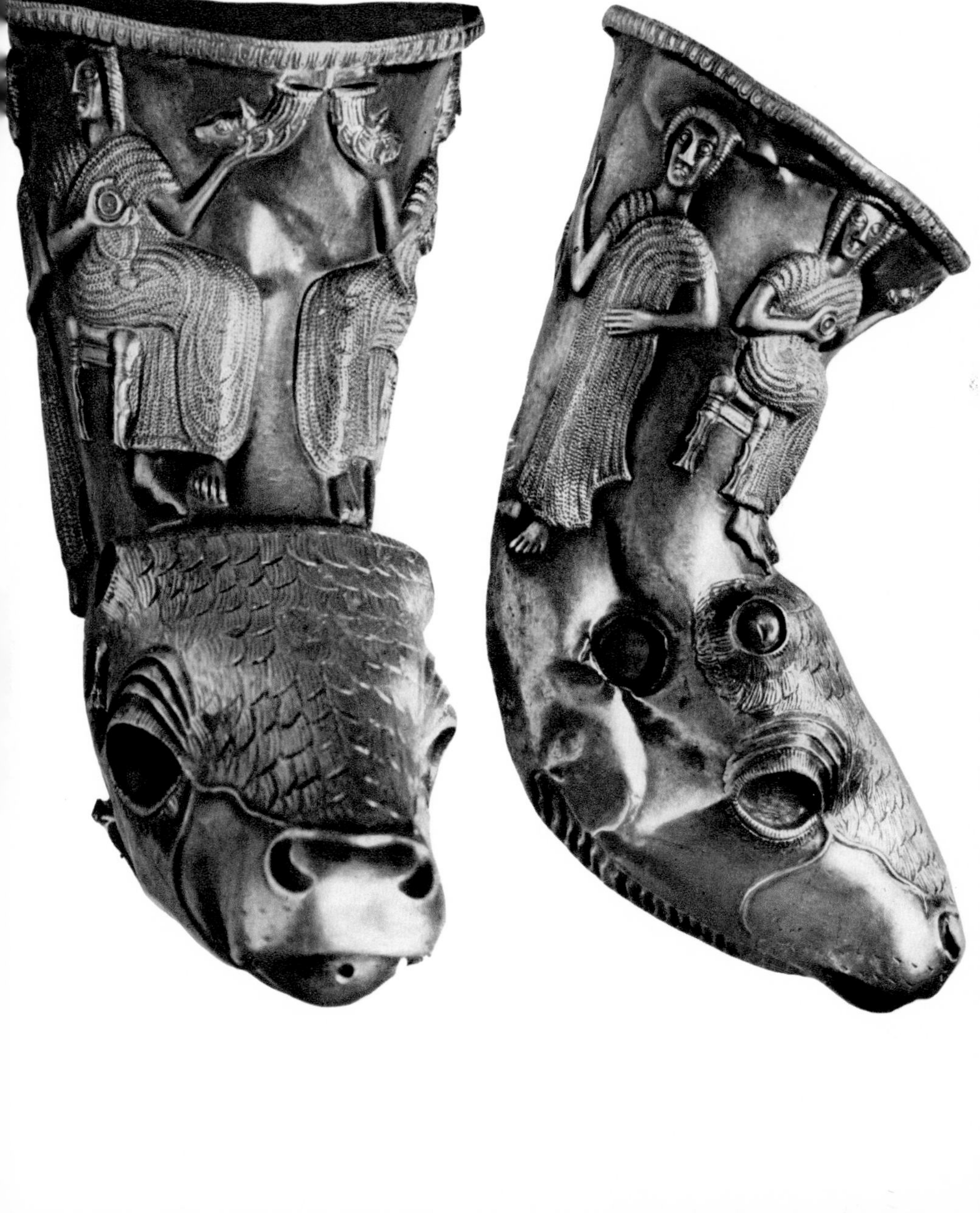

65

66

67

68

69

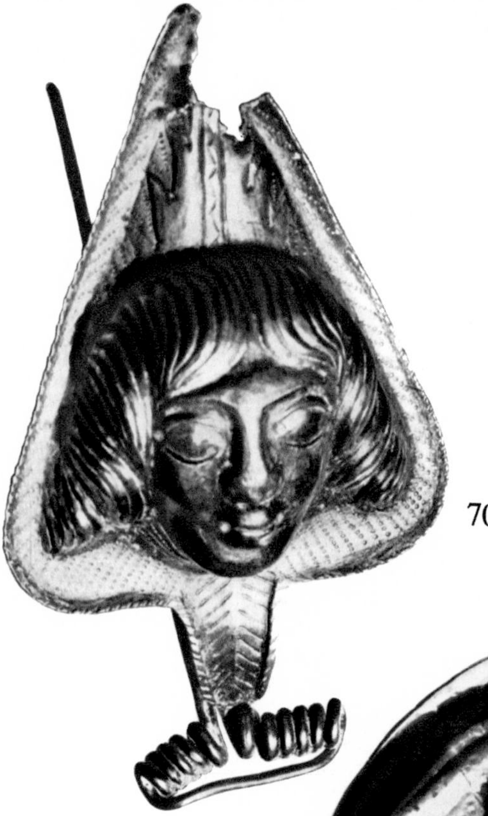

70

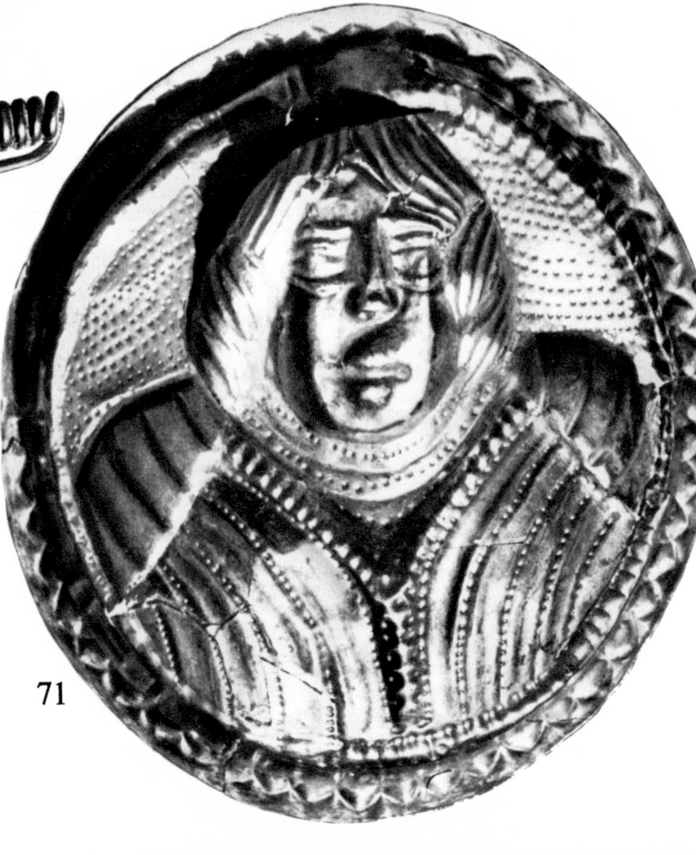

71

72

73

Notes on the Plates

1 Two Hamangia jars found in the Cernavoda cemetery. AIB.

2 Polished stone axes from the Cernavoda cemetery; Hamangia culture. Length of bottom left-hand axe 78 mm., others to scale. AIB.

3, 4 The Cernavoda 'Thinker'; Hamangia culture. Height 11.5 cm. AIB.

5 Female figurine from Cernavoda found in the same tomb as the 'Thinker'. Height 11.4 cm. AIB.

6 Hamangia baked clay figurines discovered at Baia-Hamangia. Height of largest figurine 12.5 cm. AIB.

7 Two stone axes from Valea Răii (Oltenia); Criş culture. Rm. Vîlcea Museum.

8 Horn sickle with microliths still embedded in the groove, found at Valea Răii; Criş culture. Length about 20 cm. Rm. Vîlcea Museum.

9 Early Vinča vessels discovered at Rast. AIB.

10 Pedestalled bowl from Verbicioara, belonging to the early phase of the Vinča culture. AIB.

11 Small Neolithic engraved tablets from Tărtăria (Transylvania); Turdaş culture. Diameter of round tablet 6 cm. Cluj Museum. (After N. Vlassa.)

12 Large bowl from Slatina; Vădastra culture. Slatina Museum.

13 Dish from Hotărani; Vădastra culture. Diameter 10 cm. Caracal Museum.

14 Spiral decorated pot from Vădastra; Vădastra culture. Height 14 cm. AIB.

15 Bowl from Slatina; Vădastra culture. Slatina Museum.

16 Vessel with 'musical note' (*Notenkopf*) decoration from Traian, Dealul Fîntînilor. AIB.

17 Large pot from Leţ (Sf. Gheorghe); Boian culture, phase II. Sf. Gheorge Museum.

18 Tisa pot from Reci. Sf. Gheorghe Museum.

19 Pedestalled bowl (*Steckdose*) from Glina, belonging to phase III of the Boian culture. Height about 30 cm. AIB.

20 Bone knife-handle found at Strihăreţ (Slatina); Sălcuţa culture. Slatina Museum.

21 Baked clay model of a Neolithic house from Văcăreşti (Bucharest); Gumelniţa phase III. Height about 25 cm. Bucharest Museum of History.

22 Pot stand found at Hîrşova, belonging to the Proto-Gumelniţa phase. Archaeological Museum, Constanţa.

23 *Askos* form Căscioarele, belonging to phase III of the Gumelniţa culture. Length 11 cm. Archaeological Museum, Bucharest.

24 Two bowls and a jar from 'Poiana în Pisc' (Caşolţ); Petreşti culture. Sibiu Museum.

25 Zoomorphic bowl from Calomfireşti (Muntenia); Gumelniţa culture. Height 10 cm. AIB.

26 Proto-Gumelniţa pedestalled dish from Hîrşova.

27 Ritual object probably used for ceremonial purposes, found in a dwelling at Truşeşti (Ţuguieta); Cucuteni I (A) culture. Max. height 1 m. AIB.

28 Polychrome painted ladle from Frumuşica; Cucuteni culture, phase IIIa. AIB.

29 Cucuteni I (A) painted ware. Pedestalled vessel from Truşeşti (Ţuguieta). Height 37 cm. AIB.

30 Painted jar from Traian; Cucuteni culture, phase II (AB). AIB.

31 a, Battle-axe with a disked butt; b, axe with an enlarged crescent-shaped butt. From the Apa hoard. Length of (a) 62 cm., of (b) 23.4 cm. AIB.

32 Spiral bronze armlet from the Apa hoard. Bronze IIIa. Length 22 cm. AIB.

33 A battle-axe of unusual shape, found in the Apa hoard. Bronze IIIa. Length 26 cm. AIB.

34 Gîrla Mare handled vessel with a stylized bird-head terminal found in the Ostrovul Mare cemetery. Height to rim 14.5 cm. Turnu-Severin Museum.

35 Handled pot from the Cîrna cemetery; Gîrla Mare culture. Height 28 cm.

36 Two decorated baked clay statuettes from Cîrna; Gîrla Mare culture. Height of left-hand statuette 15.6 cm., of the other 17.8 cm.

37 Channel-decorated vessel from cemetery 2 at Sărata Monteoru; Monteoru culture, phase II (Nestor's Ia). AIB.

38 Vessel for ritual offerings found in cemetery I at Sărata Monteoru; Monteoru culture phase III (Nestor's II). AIB.

39 Ornamental gold buttons from Ţigănaşi treasure; Gîrla Mare culture. Diameter of large buttons about 3 cm. Bucharest Museum of History.

40 Handled vessel with ram's-head terminal found in a hut at Sărata Monterou; Monterou culture, phase III (Nestor's IIA).

41 Inhumation burial, cemetery 2, Sărata Monteoru; Monteoru culture, phase II (Nestor's Ia). Excavations by I. Nestor.

42 Gold foil worked in repoussé and folded into a cylindrical shape, from the Poarta Albă treasure hoard (Dobrudja). About 136 cm high. National Hungarian Museum, Budapest.

43 Bronze *tutuli* (unit of money) and bangles from the Pecica hoard. (After E. Comşa.) Archaeological Museum, Constanța.

44 Large urn from the Pecica hoard; Hallstatt Ia (AI). National Hungarian Museum, Budapest.

45 A Noua-type pot with two handles found at Mediaş. Height 19 cm. AIB.

46 Dalja-type vessel from Lechința. Height 10.8 cm. AIB.

47 Large jar found at Reci; Early Hallstatt (I). Sf. Gheorge Museum.

48 Pottery of the Vîrtop horizon (second channelled-ware horizon), found at Vîrtop and Plopşor. Height of largest pot 75 cm. Craiova Museum.

49 The Lechința 'flock' of zoomorphic figurines from the Hallstatt period. Between 3 and 5.5 cm. long. AIB.

50 Vessel of the Noua type from Lechința. Height 19 cm. AIB.

51 Handled bowl from a Hallstatt grave at Cernavoda. Height 11.4 cm. AIB.

52 Cylindrical barrel-jar from Lechința; Hallstatt I. Height 50 cm. AIB.

53 Urn with lugs from tomb IV at Cernavoda belonging to the Thraco-Getian La Tène civilization. Height 41 cm. Archaeological Museum, Constanța.

54, 55 Two jugs recovered from a tomb at Cernavoda. AIB.

56 Silver anthropomorphic greave from the Thraco-Getian tomb at Agighiol (Dobrudja); Thraco-Getian La Tène civilization. Height 47.8 cm. AIB.

57 Front and side view of the gold ceremonial helmet from Coţofăneşti, belonging to the Thracian civilization. Height 25 cm. AIB.

58 Silver objects from the so-called 'Craiova treasure'; Thraco-Getian La Tène civilization. AIB.

59 The upper part of an emblem-ornament shaped like an *akinakes* from Medgidia (Dobrudja), belonging to the Thraco-Getian La Tène civilization. Total length of emblem 46.7 cm. AIB.

60, 61 Silver vessel from the tumulus grave of a Tracian *basileus* at Agighiol.

62–64 Rhyton from Poroina; an example of Thraco-Getian art.

65 Hellenistic amphora found in a Getian tomb at Zimnicea. AIB.

66 Getian wheel-made ware from Poiana; an example of Thraco-Getian art. AIB.

67 Large urn of the Dacian La Tène period found at Ocniţa (Oltenia). Height exceeds 50 cm. Rm. Vîlcea Museum.

68 Wheel-made jar from Zimnicea, belonging to the Thraco-Getian La Tène civilization. AIB.

69 Wheel-made pedestalled bowl found in the Getian cemetery at Murighiol. AIB.

70 Dacian silver mask fibula. Length 25 cm. Bucharest Museum of History.

71 Gilded silver button-fibula showing the portrait of a man found at Bucharest (Herăstrău) and datable to the first century BC. Diameter 9.2 cm. Bucharest Museum of History.

72 Silver Geto-Dacian coins discovered south of the Carpathians. Diameter about 2.3 cm. (After B. Mitrea.)

73 Celtic helmet from Ciumeşti. Height 25 cm. Cluj Museum.

Index